THE CAREER SUCCESS AND RESPONSIBLE ADULT 2-IN-1 COMBO PACK

PROVEN METHODS FOR CHOOSING A CAREER AND FINDING HAPPINESS AND SUCCESS IN ADULTHOOD

BUKKY EKINE-OGUNLANA

TCECPUBLISHING.COM

this document, including, but not limited to,—errors, omissions, or inaccuracies.

Published by

TCEC Publishing

TCEC House

14-18 Ada Street, London Fields,

E8 4QU, England, Great Britain.

CONTENTS

THE CAREER SUCCESS FORMULA

THE MOTIVATED YOUNG ADULT'S GUIDE TO CAREER SUCCESS AND ADULTHOOD

THE CAREER SUCCESS FORMULA

PROVEN CAREER DEVELOPMENT ADVICE AND
FINDING REWARDING EMPLOYMENT FOR
YOUNG ADULTS AND COLLEGE GRADUATES

DEDICATION

This lovely book is dedicated to all the beautiful students all over the world who, over the years, have passed through the T.C.E.C young adult's program. Thanks for the opportunity to serve you and invest in your colorful and bright future.

Your free gift!

Voucher ID: NGH0001

As a way of saying thank you for purchasing this book, I am offering you a free gift at the end of the book

INTRODUCTION

Are you looking for a potential career fresh out of university? Are you a professional looking to switch to a different career stream? Or perhaps you are a young adult on the hunt for the perfect job. If you fall into any of these categories or can relate to any of these scenarios in some capacity, then this book is right for you.

Finding a career that suits your interests, passions, needs, and lifestyle can be a very daunting task, specifically if you are fresh out of school. With this book, you will understand what makes a career, why it can sometimes be frustrating when you do not get the job you want, and what you can do to land a promising career as a fresh graduate young adult.

We generally define a career as a person's job during their working life. This definition is broad and includes changes such as the acquisition of skills and qualifications.

Usually, however, we associate a lot more with a career than that, namely advancement, not only in the hierarchy of a company but also socially. That means a higher position, more salary, a better company car, a more excellent office, etc. When we talk about someone who has made a career, we often imagine an absolute high-flyer with the best degrees, a quick promotion, and a résumé with whom international head-hunters would strike immediately.

The career is an individual's metaphorical "journey" through learning, work and other aspects of life. There are several ways to define a career, and the term is used in various ways. It is an omnipresent topic, not only in our career bible but in school, during studies, or in everyday life: careers are planned, discussed, and highlighted everywhere. Everyone wants to have a career, be successful, and achieve something. Few, however, think about what that means: making a career. The way is not prescribed; it does not always have to go up steeply.

Much more importantly: a career is what you make of it and what you expect from it. We show what makes a career and what possibilities there are to shape your career.

Finding a career that suits you and fulfills all of your needs may take some trial and error, which instills fear in many people because of the uncertainty that lies ahead. While it can be a stress-inducing situation, it is essential to overcome the negative outlook you may have on this journey and develop an attitude that seeks to fulfill yourself and your future truly.

This is better clearly said than done, but an excellent way to look at this is by approaching your career with creativity in mind. It is essential to think about your work's impact and its effect on those around you. This approach of coloring outside the lines, rather than falling into the structure and rules that limit you in the workplace, often yields better results. People are less afraid to take risks and truly challenge themselves in the workplace. This can mean taking on more tasks or responsibilities, branching out into other areas of interest, or even merely reaching out to those around them and being more outspoken in social situations. This differs from one person to another person and is based on their job and what it entails. But that is not to say that creativity will carry you to new heights if you keep it in mind with every task you do.

The underlying idea behind being creative with your career lies in this Jewish phenomenon: "With your certificate, you must learn another trade." Humans are multifaceted and capable of accomplishing so much more than we might think and anticipate. The circumstances that affect our lives can hit us when we are least expecting it, thus changing the course of our lives dramatically, career included. Because you can be displaced at any time, the important thing is to continually evolve and challenge yourself to acquire more skills so that you can carve a career path that truly fits you and what fascinates you, no matter what variables shape your life. The mantra is to "always be a student" because there will always be new skills to be mastered and learn. This mindset prepares you for the unknown and often spurs on burgeoning entrepreneurial spirits that most people do not realize they have.

I once discussed this with a friend of mine who was a lawyer. He had experienced a dramatic shift in life that inspired some of the basis for this book. He said the words: "These hands have provided for my necessities," which were tremendously profound and inspiring. He had attended an Ivy League law school and worked at a top law firm in Chicago. Despite having an incredibly successful career by most standards, he no longer went to court as a lawyer because he found that it was no longer a fulfilling job. What was once a role that fueled his passions for helping people become a high-strung environment that valued monetary gain above all else. Disillusioned, he ended up quitting and finding success in making tents, a newly acquired hobby that found him tapping into an entrepreneurial spirit he never knew he had.

While his career change was dramatic and certainly drastic for many, the vital thing to note here is that he did not feel limited at any point because he was always bearing the idea of a higher purpose. While giving up his law career was a huge step, he found fulfillment by staying true to his talents of helping others. He understood that burying his talents deprived others of his creations.

As the world's populace continues to grow and shows no signs of slowing down, more jobs are being cut. With technology replacing a good portion of the working sector every year, an individual's career prospects continue to diminish. The future is looking increasingly bleak for job seekers, which leaves plenty of room for job creators, entrepreneurs, and the likes of people who use their skills to make products and services that serve society. But the challenge lies in carving out a niche. How does one even begin to find a need and create a sustainable job and provide a living? One of the best strategies to do so is to expose yourself to knowledge every day and find new skills to grasp the services and products that the world does not know it needs.

Everyone is familiar with career, but hardly anyone knows where the word comes from. The term comes from the French carrière, which means something like racing track or career. Precisely what characterizes what we mean by today's career: We are in the race, are in constant competition, must give 120 percent, the others depend upon. Higher, faster, further and more successful.

A professional career can be designed and realized in many ways. Often only financial factors are taken into account to assess how successful the occupation is. However, that alone is not enough and ignores other factors such as personal satisfaction and fulfillment.

To make the diversity of the career clearer to you, this book will show you various careers and opportunities:

LEADERSHIP CAREER

This form describes what is classically understood as making a career. You work your way up in a company, climb the career ladder step by step, become a leader and take on significant responsibility. For teams, for projects, for entire companies, when you become a top manager. In a management career, a career means a position at the top, very high pay, and social advancement, which relates to the professional.

PROFESSIONAL CAREER

A professional career is not necessarily about hierarchical advancement in the profession but about becoming an expert in your field. So, you do not strive for managerial responsibility but steadily develop your qualifications, acquire in-depth know-how and have a knowledge advantage over other employees and competitors. In this way, you will become a sought-after and valuable expert highly valued by employers and negotiate a fair salary accordingly.

INDEPENDENCE

You can make a career not only with an employer but also with your own company. In self-employment, you can set up your own business, implement an idea or make a dream come true. At the same time, you become your boss, but you also bear a greater risk. Many people appreciate the greater freedom in a self-employed career because you are not bound by strict guidelines and instructions from the boss. Instead, you can make your own decisions.

FREELANCER

As a freelancer, you offer your services and skills to companies and other clients. You also enjoy greater freedom because a company does not directly employ you. On the other hand, you always must receive new orders; otherwise, no payments will be accepted. Besides, freelancers are not active and in demand in all industries.

PROJECT CAREER

The so-called project career lies somewhere between a freelancer and a specialist career. With your extensive knowledge in a specific area, you will work on projects and sometimes even lead them, but an employer or client will only employ you for the project's duration.

EMPLOYEE

In this context, one often finds the phrase: someone is only an employee. This shows the wrong view because even an employee can have a successful and promising career according to their imagination. Not everyone focuses on their job in life; some want a better work-life balance and do not want to work overtime every day to advance. As an employee in a position that makes you happy, you have exactly the career that suits you.

THE GOAL IN MIND

However, one essential aspect seems to be missing from this general definition. After all, what if you have not got where you wanted to go professionally? Those who do not exhaust their potential remain completely below their possibilities, find their tasks boring, and are permanently dissatisfied, sooner or later lose their motivation to work and identify with their job. Such a person is unlikely to claim to have made a career.

Career expert and founder of the office for career strategy, Jürgen Hesse, says: "In our daily advice, we repeatedly experience that the delighted employees are those who have achieved their project. I would make a career describe as a state of affairs that, looking back, clarifies that I have already successfully taken this professional development. Here I am and see a worthwhile, professional goal right in front of my eyes, which I will certainly achieve very soon." So, it is about a professional goal you have set yourself. And that can turn out very differently - whether you want to become a gardener, space researcher, department head, or independent management consultant. The two crucial questions are always: What is your goal, and how do you get there?

Those who can no longer put their personal goals into practice need to compare themselves with others and their professional life courses. However, some people do not even know exactly what their future careers should look like. So what? After all, you can only follow your path if you know where it should lead you. So, first find out what you want and above all think about your competencies, your talents, abilities and skills, your professional and personal interests and inclinations.

A seminar on potential analysis can help you to get on track with yourself and your wishes. With this changed perspective on careers, Angela Sommer suddenly finds it very easy to look forward to her class reunion. Because she has achieved exactly what she always wanted - she does exactly the job that she enjoys and gives her time to her family. So, if a former classmate asks her: "What are you doing?" She will answer very simply and confidently: "I've made a career."

RETHINKING CAREER

But change is slowly taking place. In the prior, it was frowned upon and associated with the weakness to take a break. You can now find "sabbaticals" or parental leave very often listed in the résumés. Fathers take time off to have time for their families, and young people are increasingly taking sabbaticals to travel the world or to rethink their previous lives.

In the meantime, many companies, especially agile organizations, see this as positive. We are not looking for perfect employees, but team members who find creative solutions with whom we enjoy working with and strive for the next highest position and meaning. An experience that is acquired outside of traditional career paths, such as a trip around the world, is essential for companies that encourage "out of the box" thinking.

People often take one more step in the Anglo-Saxon world: so-called "zigzag" CVs are not uncommon but regular. While (supposedly) secure jobs and careers are still upheld in Germany, Americans, for example, look around much more often for new jobs and sometimes go more unconventional ways than we are used to in the country. Of course, financial aspects are in the foreground due to the low coverage and personal development level. While it is complicated to switch to controlling in Germany after years of marketing experience, this is not uncommon in other countries. Or it is normal to have worked as a barista in the meantime.

INDIVIDUAL CAREER PATHS AND DEVELOPMENT OPPORTUNITIES

This is nice because you may only discover unrecognized talents or potentials once you have tried something different. Or it confirms that the current job is precisely right for you. For me, a career is much more than climbing a ladder (and that usually leads to the top), but rather a development. A development process in which you recognize strengths, develop talents, and thus assemble your career path.

I am a certified career coach myself. Working with Young Adults, but I am not 100% happy with this. Because even during the apprenticeship, there were so many topics that you might not associate with the title. It was much more about development areas, how these can be addressed, identified, and then implemented in the job. How to recognize and achieve goals, arrive on the job market, but not with yourself.

Classic careers will continue to exist, just like people who have detailed résumés and are treated as "aspiring employees" or "high potentials." And that is just as well! Such people naturally have entirely different issues when they turn to me than at a crossroads. But they too have careers, but the definition may be different, and so are the topics in the coaching process.

After reading this book, please feel free to leave a review based on your findings and how useful the book was to you. I would be incredibly thankful if you could take 60 seconds to write a brief review on the platform of purchase, even if it's just a few sentences!

HOW TO MAKE A CAREER CHOICE

*P*eople mostly have problems based on their career planning strategies and choice making. Knowledge base comes from knowing what job is right for you and test to see what career is best for you.

Today we face an incredible number of opportunities to develop professionally. That is wonderful. It offers a chance to live out our various talents. At the same time, it also raises the pressure to find an area, an industry, an activity that fulfills us, if possible, until the end of our (professional) life and in that case "to make a career," that is, to advance us.

My opinion: We no longer need to submit to this pressure today. We can actively and independently shape what a career is for us and how we want to shape it. More in the sense of a trade which is winding and with a depth that we have designed for ourselves. If you have that, then go for it.

With thousands of opportunities, how will you choose a career that is right for you? If you do not know what you want to do, the task may seem impossible. Fortunately, it is not. Follow organized proceedings, and you will increase your chances of making the right decision.

Plenty of people have graduated from college and entered the workforce to find out that their skillset and interests would be better suited in a different field that requires additional schooling. Going back to college at the non-typical college age is perfectly acceptable. It is, in fact, commendable because it shows that you are frequently willing to challenge yourself and evolve as an individual to find your niche and promote your efforts in a field that would better suit it.

So, take note of this in your mind that if you are a young adult struggling to find where you might thrive. The world is your oyster, and the privileges seem limitless because they are. There are so many opportunities out there if you truly take your time to research and educate yourself on the prospects that lie ahead of you. Remember that your decision at eighteen years old does not define the trajectory of the rest of your life. Career changes are regular and part of life. Ultimately, you have to prioritize yourself and put your needs above societal expectations.

ASSESS YOURSELF

Before you can choose the right profession, you must learn about yourself. Your values, interests, soft skills, and aptitudes, combined with your makeup or personality type, make some occupations a good fit for you and others completely inappropriate. While you are still in university, always look up job prospects. You need to check yourself on what you want. The goal is to take a deep dive into yourself to consider everything that has struck a chord with you in your life to go about deciding if this is something you want to pursue when you age. This is also the perfect time to try out internships or part-time jobs. While many of these positions might be unpaid, the experience you receive in return is precious and can help you figure out where you might want to focus your efforts.

Use self-assessment tools and trade tests to gather information about your traits and, subsequently, generate a list of lines of works that are the best fit based on them. Some individuals choose to work with a career counselor or other career development professionals who can help them navigate this process.

For some people, figuring out their career path is a no-brainer. School years can facilitate strengths like mathematics and science that lead to career paths in technology or medicine. For others, the answer is not so simple and might take ample trial and error to find the best fit for them. Whichever route you have taken, remember that there is no wrong answer.

MAKE A LIST OF OCCUPATIONS TO EXPLORE

You possibly have multiple lists of lines of works in front of you at this point—one generated by any of the self-assessment tools or mechanism you used. To keep yourself organized, you shall combine them into one master list.

First, look for careers that show on multiple lists and copy them onto a blank page. Title or label it "Occupations to Explore." Your self-assessments indicated they are an acceptable fit for you based on several of your traits, so they are worth exploring.

Next, find occupations or work on your lists that appeal to you. They can be careers you know a bit about and want to explore further. Also, include professions about which you do not know much. You might learn something unexpected.

EXPLORE THE OCCUPATIONS ON YOUR LIST

At this point, you will be thrilled you managed to narrow your list down to only 10 to 20 options. Now you can get some necessary information about each of the occupations on your list.

Find job descriptions, educational training, and licensing requirements in published sources. Learn about leading opportunities. Use government-produced labor market knowledge to get data about earnings and job outlook.

CREATE A "SHORT LIST"

Now you have more knowledge, start to narrow down your list table even further. Based on what you studied from your investigation so far, begin eliminating the careers you do not want to pursue any further. You will end up with two to five lines of works or crafts on your "shortlist."

If your reasons for finding a line of work unacceptable are non-negotiable, cross it off your list. Eliminate everything with duties that do not appeal to you. Eliminate professions that have weak job outlooks. Get rid of any line of work if you are unable or unwilling to fulfill the educational or other requirements or if you lack some of the soft skills necessary to succeed in it.

Shortlisting careers is essential to not end up with a job that makes you feel constant frustration and regret later.

Take the time to research and put effort into considering the careers that interest you. While it is not permanent, it will be a substantial commitment to finally decide on the trades that pique your interest.

CONDUCT INFORMATIONAL INTERVIEWS

When you have only a few occupations or works left on your list, begin doing a more in-depth analysis. Arrange a meet-up with people who work in the professions in which you are interested. They can provide firsthand knowledge about the job on your shortlist. Access your network, including LinkedIn, to find individuals with whom to have these informational interviews.

You can also check out job reviews on these careers online or ask others what they think. It is good to have input from other people, especially those working in these careers. This will help you get an idea of what to expect from them. You can also approach your professors or mentors in university to gauge their inputs on these careers.

This is also the gateway to networking. This helps develop some lasting relationships that can help your career trajectory later on in life, whether you seek to advance your career or completely take a different pathway. In-depth research and making connections with like-minded people can broaden the horizon and expose you to jobs you might have never considered.

Furthermore, networking from a young age prepares you later on in your career, when you have to face more seniors and executives. Having the experience can set you apart from coworkers and competition because you are seasoned and well-prepared with the expertise needed to meet these high-intensity situations.

MAKE YOUR CAREER CHOICE

Lastly, after doing all your research, you are probably ready to make your choice. Pick the occupation you think will bring you the most satisfaction based on all the information you have gathered. Realize that you are allowed to do-overs if you change your mind about your choice at any point in your life. A lot of people change their careers at least a few times.

Remember that this is just your initial career. Do not expect that this will be your only career in life unless you want it to be. You can change jobs as much as you want in the future. But that does not also mean that you slack off. You still have to do your best once you start working.

IDENTIFY YOUR GOALS

Once you make a choice, identify your long- and short-term goals. This will help to chart a course toward eventually landing work in your decided field. Long-term objectives typically take about three to five years to reach, while you can usually fulfill a short-term purpose in six months to about three years.

Let the research you did about required schooling, education, and training be your guide. If you do not have all the specifics, do some more research. Once you have all the data you need, set your goals. An example of a long-term objective would be completing your schooling and training. Short-term objectives include applying to college, apprentice-ships, other training programs, and internships.

Having more significant, overarching goals can help you home in on the finer details that are often more difficult to iron out. Bigger goals help define the direction you want to go in because it is the first step needed to figure out important details like your major in college or an internship you might find worthwhile pursuing.

WRITE A CAREER ACTION PLAN

Put together a progressive career action plan, a written document that lays out all the steps or tracks you will have to take to reach your objectives. Visualize it as a road map that can take you from point A to B, then to C and D. Pen down all your short- and long-term objectives and the steps you will have to take to reach each one. Add any anticipated barriers that could get in the way of achieving your dreams— and the ways you can overcome them.

MEET WITH AN ADVISOR

If you are in school, this is the perfect time to take advantage of all of the career advisors and counselors that are specifically put in place to help you figure out your needs. Even without a solid plan, career advisors can help you develop a plan to put into motion. This way, if you are in school and trying to figure out what to major in, you will fulfill all of the prerequisites required to give yourself options when the time comes to make a final decision on what exactly you intend to pursue.

Use the resources available

Take advantage of your school's events that get you connected with industry professionals who have experience with recruiting and internships. Getting advice directly from the source is tremendously valuable and can offer insight into whether this career path you have chosen is the best fit for you. It is essential to ask the right questions and get the most transparent and honest answers, and these advisors are here specifically to do so.

Despite your research and networking efforts, you might find that deciding on a career that fits all of your interests is very difficult. Many students face this and leave their majors undeclared until the last minute. When graduation arrives, these young adults panic and make last-minute decisions on their careers that they later regret. You may not believe me, but this too is par for the course.

For some, this might indicate that you may have to carve out your niche to create a career that truly suits your interests, goals, and ambitions in life. Gaining new skills and experience is the way to do this. Perhaps you still need foundational knowledge in a broad subject like a business to tap into your entrepreneurial side. Or maybe interning in areas that interest you can help you draw inspiration for your own business.

And for many others, this might be a sign that having real-life experience will indeed give the final push into a particular direction to make a more well-informed decision. Many young adults choose to intern and work in various positions as soon as they graduate to explore career options in a more hands-on way.

This may sound like it is a lot of work—and it is. But it is a lot easier to forge a career route when you know what you wish. Taking these steps initially will save you many trials, struggles, and uncertainty in the long run.

HOW TO KNOW IF YOU'VE CHOSEN THE WRONG CAREER

There are quite a minority of tell-tale signs that indicate if the career path you are in is not the right one for you. Many people can tell as soon as they step foot into their workplace on the first day and observe other team members' dynamics. But quitting a job can be tremendously intimidating because it brings uncertainty and anxiety about finding your next one, and many people choose to stick it out because they simply do not have the luxury to quit. Bills have to be paid, and making a living is more important than finding fulfillment, right?

Wrong. Compromising yourself, your beliefs, and your values for a job can be extremely draining for an individual. Going to work every day with people you do not like can be extremely demotivating and demoralizing. These factors have an immense impact on your quality of life and can take a significant toll on your mental health and stability. If you find that you are faced with these feelings, it might be time to begin the transition process in your job, perhaps to a different department, role, or altogether a different route.

Indicators that it might be such a time to quit your job:

- Your work is not challenging nor fulfilling. Instead, you find yourself feeling drained every time, and you have a negative outlook on your work, regardless of how well you have executed it. This negative outlook can

manifest into a mindset that affects your
entire day and drags you down.

- Your strengths are never utilized. Completing
your work is a constant uphill battle, and you
find yourself not being able to take
advantage of your unique skillset in your
professional life.

- You are too comfortable in your position.
While most people aspire for comfort and
having confidence when it comes to their
jobs, you can have too much of a good thing.
If you find that you are not being challenged
in any way, this might be the time to move
onto something with higher stakes. Being
able to push yourself to learn and grow is one
of the most critical parts of a career.

- Lack of promotions. Sometimes being too
comfortable in your position indicates that it
is time to move onto a more prominent role.
But suppose your company does not support
growth or facilitate your experience by
giving you more responsibilities. This can
lead to a sense of stagnation that makes you
feel restless and dissatisfied.

- You have given your job 110%. You cannot
possibly dedicate any more time or energy,

given that you are one individual trying to ensure the best results every time. Yet, you find that you are unfulfilled, and your results are never as good as you would like. This could indicate that this career you have chosen is not a good fit for you, and it might be time to move onto something different.

- You find yourself unsatisfied with the industry. Perhaps it is the unruly behavior that is allowed, like workplace harassment or discrimination. Or maybe it is a work culture that has been normalized, where it is toxic and extremely harmful for your mental health. This is a massive sign that the industry does not align with your personal beliefs, and you need to move on to something else.

- You are bringing home the negativity. It is one thing to have a bad day at work. But once you start bridging that same negative mindset into your household, you begin to affect those around you inadvertently.

- You feel suffocated. This can be the case for many creatives who do not realize that their passions lie in them thinking outside of the

box rather than subscribing to another
corporate cog.

- Continually thinking about quitting might be
  a more significant sign than you think. Take
  time to seriously consider why you are
  always contemplating quitting your job and
  weighing the pros and cons.

areers do not fall from the sky. Even with a little bit of hard work and perseverance, the journey is far from over. Is the next or later step on the career ladder long overdue? Then it is time to take your career development into your own hands. Here are eight tips for your professional advancement.

"Building a career" means more than a raise in salary

Behind the concept of professional success, there are very different definitions and understandings of career. However, this refers to the professional career in general, which includes aspects of salary, the classic "ascending" hierarchies in a company, and the assumption of responsibility. However, a digital market survey and opinion research survey show more to a career than money and power—more than 75% name the aspect of professional freedom as a distinguishing feature of a successful career. Space of decision and flexible working hours, and an excellent work-life balance are part of a successful - and healthy - career. The enjoyment of the job, the individual self-realization, and the personal level of awareness in the own branch are ranked higher than the status of the salary and the company hierarchy's rank.

I used to think that making a career means finding a clear path, very determined, and quickly. Today I define "career" very differently.

"CAREER" MEANS HAVING CONSTANT PRESSURE

I put myself under pressure for a long time. It was so important to me to have a career that shines and sparkles on the outside. With which I can impress and which my family can proudly talk about. Today, I could let go of this claim and follow my vision of an authentic career. I ask myself the following questions:

What does it mean to have a trade? And what should your job look like?

And I am sure that young adults like you also have these expectations and are asking the same questions. Today I am at a point where I know: work is part of my life, and at the same time, work is not my life. Just a few years ago, I found it hard to imagine finding recognition and acceptance when I am not productive, cannot show significant results, and when I am just there.

I still love creating things and being successful, but for different reasons. It used to be elementary for me to have a job that makes my family proud and calms them down and is therefore associated with a good salary (my fallacy: a lot of money = a lot of recognition = more excellent personal value). From today's perspective, of course, my choice of profession for finance can also be questioned in terms of acceptance and recognition, but ten years ago, it promised a successful career. And that is what I wanted, right?

WHAT MAKES SUCCESSFUL PEOPLE?

Varied factors and character traits can facilitate a career boost. In particular, people with a very self-confident demeanor, the right specialist knowledge, a strong passion for the industry, and a thriving network, have the best starting career opportunities. But that character traits and soft skills will help you achieve happiness in your career? In general, however, the study of market and opinion research identified the following characteristics and traits as career pushes:

- Communication skills
- Resilience
- Professional competence
- Power of decision
- Self-confidence
- Determination
- Conflict resolution skills
- Sense of responsibility
- Reliability

The characteristics that appear further down in the ranking that should not be underestimated include social skills: teamwork and critical skills, empathy or integrity, and honesty. Nevertheless, a certain amount of self-marketing and self-staging is required in most industries and positions for a career kick, which gives some people a significant advantage by their nature - regardless of talent.

WHAT DOES IT MEAN TO HAVE A SUCCESSFUL CAREER?

The term career is completely unspectacular on its own and is defined as follows (see Wikipedia):

1. A person's career is his professional life, sober and unbiased
2. Every operational sequence of positions of a person in a functional structure, technical and value-free.

WHAT IS A RELAXED DEFINITION OF CAREER?

I like to see a career as a person's career in their professional life and view it more neutrally. This leaves the space open for many creative options for personal career decisions. Because while when you think of a career, you often think of an ascending staircase, a career path can be winding, branching off, going up and down, turning a loop, just like (professional) life.

The supposed ideal career: school, studies/training that are fun, a job that suits me well and is fulfilling, advancement in this job that suits me so well, money, influence, leadership, is only granted to a few. Lucky guys?

CAN A CAREER ALSO BE CALLED A CAREER?

Decide for yourself. Whether you are still in university, a fresh graduate, or a young adult on their first leg of job search, you need to ask these questions:

- Can your career have a career character?
- Is it okay if you have studied business administration and discover that your heartbeat is for social education?
- Do you want to attempt a different branch of your company?
- Can you start another degree? Can you create your own business?
- Can you switch back to a permanent position from self-employment?

I have grappled with similar questions about my career. And it was good to give permission finally to myself: Yes, I can. I can try things out, and I can make new turns and follow them. And if I get to a dead-end, I can turn around and take another turn—none of this changes anything about my worth. I only win—experience, knowledge, and contacts. It would be best if you did the same.

COURAGE PAYS OFF

Asking yourself these questions takes courage and perseverance. Changing your choices before you grab onto a specific career takes time. You will have to prepare things, make contacts, write applications, and face setbacks. Your acquaintances, friends, and family will question your decisions, mostly because they want to protect you (and maybe themselves) and because they mean well with you.

8 TIPS FOR A CAREER

Anyone who has wished to pursue a career for a long time and has stagnated may have been in the same job at the same company for some time—the same thing with fresh graduates. You may have thought of your ideal career for so long that you end up missing out on other opportunities because you are settled with your "ideal" job.

Do not forget that good chances of a higher career level have people whose professional context is changing - such as when a job changes. Ideally, you will go through an average of three to four job changes up to your career's peak to gain different professional experience and still not lose a sure consistency in your job. With these eight tips for starting a career, your professional happiness comes one step closer:

Importance of career: First, make yourself aware that professional advancement is for you personally. One is often strongly influenced by social ideals and career paths customary in the industry and thereby loses sight of individual career happiness.

1. **Goodbye perfectionism**: If you set yourself too high a standard, you will never meet your criteria. The pursuit of perfection instantly ends in frustration and demotivation. Recognize your strengths but also your learning areas and stay successful in this way.

2. **Mistakes = valuable experience**: The schooling fields also include reflecting on small and large errors. The aim here is to

understand that mistakes are valuable enrichment for you. This is the only way to make progress in terms of soft and hard skills. That means gaining experience - no matter what! Your self-presentation and rhetorical skills do not necessarily work naturally as a career starter. Here, you need to learn from your mistakes and get the best out of your talent. This will eventually help you as you search for the right job.

3. **Flexible strategies**: Many ways lead to the goal. Do not stick to a single path to your dream job; keep several options open - including a possible career as a career change. Define areas and strategies and use them flexibly, depending on the situation and company. Those who remain flexible in their requirements also have better cards in salary and job negotiations.

4. **Defeat habits**: Everyone has "bad habits" that make it difficult for themselves or others somehow. Postponing annoying tasks, regularly arriving late at meetings, being unreliable in keeping promises, etc., should never be cultivated. The first step is when you look at your bad habits. Do not let them

get in your way. Discard old habits through self-discipline.

5. **Initiate and do not wait**: You must act to achieve your goals. Do not wait until you are offered a career opportunity. Take the initiative yourself - for example, an internship change abroad. If you wish to make a career, you must take responsibility for yourself. Individuals who act independently focus on opportunities and do not worry about guilt when something does not go according to plan. Careerists ask themselves: what could I have done differently or better? Take on the problem and refrain from justifying yourself. Regular Staff meetings with your supervisor will also help towards your career.

6. **Invest in networks**: You climb the career ladder step by step. You can also observe this when other role models and careers inspire you in similar industries. Research possible contact points with people who share your interests: Lectures, conferences, and trade fairs are excellent opportunities to get to know people in a small group. Caution: Don't network just for the sake of networking! A

sizeable online network on Xing or LinkedIn is by no means a guarantee of success. Quality before quantity!

7. **"No" to the decision dilemma**: People who put decisions on the back burner and let themselves be drifted lose respect both for others and for themselves. Some people do not want to decide out of uncertainty. Of course, this means that the decision will be made for you by someone else. Again and again, critics and pessimists will cross your career path. Do not let their negative attitudes infect you. Believe in yourself and your abilities!

The pressure to have a successful career is a real and tangible aspect of entering the workforce. The pressure to grind and get into the nitty-gritty of working to succeed is continuously being forced onto young adults because this is the work culture that we have established as the norm. But "success" in itself can mean a lot of different things for many other people. For some, success looks like a certain amount of money in their bank account. Some view success as being able to own a house. At the same time, some see success as a state of mind rather than material goods, where success is peace of mind from worries.

One thing is exact, "success" varies from person to person. When it comes down to the real it, it is up to you to decide what you want to amount to in your lifetime. Societal pressures will continue to exist and challenge you down to your core but stay true to your ambitions and goals.

This was abundantly clear when I had a conversation with a young entrepreneur who had just graduated from college. At the age of twenty- four, he had sold off his first tech company in a seven-figure deal. He was set for life. Yet upon speaking to him, it was evident that the money was not his primary concern like it would have been for most young adults of his age. Instead, he was already developing his next piece of technology that he hoped would be implemented in schools all across the country. He was incredibly transparent when he shared that the money was exciting at first. Still, the real excitement lay that now he could fund his passions, making educational teaching accessible and affordable. Aside from being a noble and impressive pursuit, it was astounding to me that this 24-year-old was not planning on blowing through his money by buying luxury cars and gadgets.

The fact is that while money seems to keep the world spinning, it cannot possibly begin to fill deep emotional voids like passion.

WOMEN AND CAREERS

areer opportunities for women have continued to improve in recent years. Nevertheless, young female professionals "to achieve anything" do not always match gender-specific professional realities. For women to advance professionally, not only the professional qualifications but especially the career-enhancing character traits must be right. Family planning can also become a significant obstacle to a career as a woman. Even if you are on maternity leave, it does not necessarily have to lead to the end of career advancement. The differences between the sexes affect women's natural reproductive role and differences in terms of care obligations after childbirth, part-time work, and income. The female employment rate in Austria has been increasing for years, with the number of women fully employed tending to stagnate. The difference in wages or salaries between women and men (gender pay gap) in Austria remains a significant career problem for women with a difference of 20% (2016) - well above the average EU gap of 16.2%.

The good news first: there have never been so many well-educated women as there are today. In terms of education, women are ahead by a nose. The proportion of women graduating from university is currently 56% in Austria and 79% in teacher training colleges.

And yet data from Statistics in Austria shows: Even if they are better educated, women still earn less than men, work more than before, and more often sit in less lucrative

Part-time positions. The sad reality is that women and men doing the same job are not playing the field.

The fact is that women often face an uphill battle, especially in specific industries that males heavily dominate. The reality is that work cultures can be a toxic and dehumanizing place for women because they are frequently up against barriers and hurdles. Women have double the challenge of having to show even more competency and professionalism than their male counterparts. The workforce can genuinely be a cesspool of sexism and discrimination for women. Most of the time, it goes unnoticed and unpunished because speaking out can be a dangerous thing not just in the moment but also for her entire career trajectory.

Women are also not nearly as represented in senior positions. The numbers for women of color in leadership positions also continue to remain low. While progress has been made in recent years, the gap continues to remain startlingly wide between the number of men in senior positions versus women. While so many factors continue to shape our workforce's statistics, it certainly brings up questions about how exactly the gap between men and women in the force has maintained itself and why improvements are moving at a snail's pace.

While there are ways for women to cope with this and try to work around the workforce's disadvantages, the sheer fact that women have to face a set of challenges that males do not encounter is unacceptable and demoralizing. The situation becomes doubly challenging with working mothers who have to deal with a full plate at work and home as well, where their children and the household awaits. Even though the support and resources to help alleviate some of the stress and responsibilities have improved in recent years, access to these resources is not universal. For many families, support is a luxury. Daycare and after-school activities can be an added financial burden that households are not ready for.

As a whole, these dynamics and competing forces are difficult to grapple with. The question or challenge that begs to be answered is how women can find careers that have a positive work environment, fit their skillset, and pay enough while also allowing them to grow and flourish as an individual? It is an incredibly complicated question that continually proves to be an impossible feat for young adults everywhere as the job market grows increasingly competitive and job security looks precarious, at best.

In the workplace and to finally succeed with a career of their own, women are often advised to be more aggressive, adopt male colleagues' habitus, and leave emotions aside to play in the "Boys Club" on the upper floor. This is often meant nicely but overlooks a severe problem: Even if women adopt all-male colleagues' behavior one-to-one, they are assessed differently. If a loud colleague is assertive and "man-agement material," a woman who gets noisy from time to time is quickly described as "bitch" and "too emotional." These assessments are wildly unfair, of course. Still, the deeper issue at hand is that it perpetuates stereotypes about women and is an unjust judge of their character as an individual.

Nevertheless, you can use a few tricks to climb the corporate ladder and sell your achievements well. How does it work? With daring, a good network, and a certain amount of audacity. This book will present to you how you can make a career.

INSIDER TIPS

1. Just do not be too hardworking.

Doing as much as possible well and diligently is still seen by many as the means of choice to attract attention in the job and be seen as a high performer. But that could be the wrong path, says executive coach Christina. She advises women to shift down a gear: "Male monocultures love female diligence because it saves them work. But from experience, I can say that diligent removal sends the wrong signals," she writes in the Handel Blatt.

Successful managers know that just 20% effort is enough to solve 80% of the problems.

Christina, therefore, advises women not to call out "here" when standard tasks are assigned. "Women are much more successful when they pick up strategically important topics or proactively develop them themselves." In this way, women build up an essential field of expertise on the job, which improves their standing and is recognized within the group. Nothing is more crucial than repeatedly pointing out your performance and putting your expertise in the spotlight.

If a female is just getting started with their job fresh from graduation, then they need to keep this in mind: "Do not be too fast on volunteering your help or working too hard to impress your bosses. Be strategic instead." The solution often lies in working smarter, not harder.

2. Women must sell themselves better

Only those who are seen win. Women should therefore use the stage whenever they are available and not skip a presentation. This requires a good deal of self-confidence - and in addition to professional competence, the security to shine and shine with your topic. The best way to do this is through repeated practice: in front of colleagues, in meetings, and in important meetings. Instead of letting others go first, women must take the floor and present themselves.

As a young adult or fresh graduate woman, you might be shy to make a presentation in the front, which should not be. Relinquish that shyness because the competition is high in a place where women should never sell themselves short.

Gone are the days where women are docile and stay hidden behind men. Women should now take a stance and aim to better themselves as well. Women should not be afraid to sell their business skills just because men dominate the industry. Skill and talent do not mind any sex or gender. What matters is if the bearer is skilled or not.

3. Take advantage of your strengths.

Everyone has strengths and weaknesses, but the important thing is that you play up to your strengths and take advantage of the skills that make you a valuable and indispensable part of the company. Working on your weaknesses on the side is an excellent strategy to improve and evolve constantly. But the key here is to put yourself out there with your strong suits and rely on them because they can set you apart from everyone else.

For women especially, it can be tempting to compare yourself with others. Comparing your success with others will only set you back and lead you down a path of self-doubt and insecurity. This can also jeopardize relationships because of how you may be projecting these insecurities onto those you are comparing yourself with.

Analyzing others can help you make practical decisions that will help your career. Rather than comparisons, take a more pragmatic approach by assessing your strengths and then assessing others and how they may add to the dynamic in their unique way. This takes the pressure off from yourself to be like your coworkers and instead focuses on the strengths that reaffirm your position and why you are a valuable member who still has room to grow.

CHARACTERISTICS OF A CAREER WOMAN

If you wish to make a career, you must have the courage to take your professional fate into your own hands and sometimes make risky decisions. Even if people keep talking about compatibility, other things inevitably remain on the job when concentrating on your career. Randi Zuckerberg knows that too. The famous Facebook founder's sister says: "Friendships, career, family, fitness or enough sleep: choose three of them. More is not possible."

Include determination and a willingness to take risks. These qualities also help to climb the corporate ladder:

- Self-discipline
- Courage to be honest
- Assertiveness
- Optimism
- flexibility
- Resilience
- Result orientation
- Openness
- Teamwork

INTERVIEW ANSWERS

What is essential is the desire to have a career

Ms. J, you claim that women appear too modest and sell themselves poorly. Why?

Cornelia J: Women often have little regard for their achievements and do not self-confidently appear as above-average performers. Women also live in more complex life situations: whether at work, as a mother, as a partner, or as a family organizer, many women want to fill all roles optimally. That takes strength. Men, on the other hand, target more on their job. This is noticed by superiors and has lots of advantages.

So, is it their fault if they fail to climb the corporate ladder?

Not exactly. But top management candidates are mostly selected by top management and owners, and most of them are men. Their perception of women in top positions is very different. Also, certain role expectations must be fulfilled in top management, for which women are often poorly prepared.

What expectations?

Fast decision-making, for example. Many male executives do not think long about the consequences of decisions, while women consider their social impact choice. Besides work, the social aspect is also essential: men spend five evenings in a row with customers, women hardly socialize after work or on the weekend. This is because they are still primarily responsible for the household - and men do too little for it.

Experts say that women in management positions bring companies forward economically. Nevertheless, only one in ten managers in Austria is female.

Classic roles continue to dominate in this country. The woman's job is still seen as a side income.

What kind of education or training do women have at work?

It is essential to have a profound desire to have a career. Women must be aware that they must do without a lot for this. That is why when a woman lands her first job after graduation; she needs to have a goal. She needs to acquire as much training as work allows because this training will help to achieve more.

Does a woman have to do more professionally than a man?

Women not only have to perform above average, but they also must sell themselves particularly well to make a career. To get into really top positions, they also must learn how to use power. In many cases, however, there is a lack of role models for this. But that does not mean that it is already time to give up with the lack of role model. No! Instead, women should strive even more to become a pioneer of that change.

In which industries do women have the best chances for a top position?

From today's perspective in service professions. This is where women are mostly socializing and are most likely to be recognized. They are service and customer-oriented, pay attention to their employee's and stakeholders' involvement, and can do many things at once - or at least that is what you believe of them.

NETWORKING FOR YOUR CAREER

Men have recognized it for centuries: their career is not decided in the office but in an informal setting. Whether in the men's toilet or at a company event, a good network is still the be-all and end-all of career planning. Here jobs and projects are assigned informally, and information is shared that bystanders do not even hear or only hear much later. Women who want to get to the top should take this to heart: In an interview with the German star, Douglas M, who calls on women to give each other suitable jobs. "Men have always supported one another. We can do that too!" Said the top manager.

Networking is not a skill that is taught at school. The real, exclusive way to get better at networking is by socializing, which we as humans get better at through experience. Networking, at its core, is a matter of allying. For women, this tends to prove more valuable and necessary than an individual's position or salary. Developing a foundation of mutual respect and trust with a group will grow into a bond that can be extremely valuable in advancing your career. Having people that you can trust in a dog-eat-dog world can make all the difference.

For both men and women, the nature of industries and work environments can often steer them into an increasingly competitive approach to climbing the ladder. Instead of uplifting others, the temptation to step on others to advance is not only tempting but a common occurrence. But doing so enables the toxic environment that continues to not only pit women against each other but also stereotypes women as ruthless, cunning, and altogether unapproachable.

This is where alliances can shape a woman's role in the industry. Having the support of others on a long-term basis can flourish into personal friendships that bleed into personal and professional lives. These contacts are not merely tools for advancing in your career but can become valuable support systems for advice and professional help. Especially in male-dominated industries, this help is central to success.

With men fully taking advantage of networking, as "Boys Only" clubs are rampant in every industry sector, women should weaponize this, just as men have to facilitate their career aspirations and needs. Having the ability to rely on a support group is one of the biggest perks of employment, no matter what industry you are in. Work culture is one of the biggest concerns when it comes to starting a new job. One of the most common questions that interviewers are asked is how the work culture is within the company. For women, this is often coded about the toxicity with other women and the dynamics between genders. It has such a profound impact on every aspect of being an employee and the work they produce. Therefore, having strong ties with like-minded people who also share the same values in terms of the workplace can propel your career and make your experience a far more positive one.

Developing contacts and allowing your qualifications to shine through which can get you into places you may never have even considered before. Networking is useful precisely for this. Building new relationships and getting your name out there exposes you to a larger pool of people who can truly broaden your horizons. This can be a daunting task, but being unafraid and putting yourself out there is the most significant part of networking. Many people fumble during their first few experiences with coffee chats because they tend to psych themselves out. There tends to be considerable stress or pressure that comes with networking, and rightfully so. For many people, the next coffee chat could mean a new opportunity like a promotion or a different position that aligns with their personal goals. You truly can never fully anticipate the extent of the options that arise out of socializing and putting yourself out there.

One of the biggest mistakes that stem from networking anxiety is that people are tempted to over-think things and feel the need to embellish themselves to sell themselves and leave a lasting impression. Ultimately, you are trying to show others your competency, enthusiasm, and qualifications in a more personable and approachable way than in a formal interview setting. This doesn't mean that you have to change your personality and pretend to be someone else entirely. You want to share your authentic self in an organic way, which is often the basis of how these conversations end up turning into networking opportunities that lead to even more options that change a person's career trajectory for the better.

You do not fundamentally have to go to evening events to network. Networking is everywhere: in the coffee kitchen, at the edge of a conference, in the fitness center, or on the playground. To get to know new perspectives and make your competence public, you can always lunch with colleagues from other departments and talk about your projects. After all, everyone is themselves an ambassador for their performance process. That does not mean showing off success at random but instead allowing your expertise to flow in where it is needed - elegantly and as if on the side.

SMART WAYS TO EXPAND YOUR NETWORK

There are also smart ways to set up and expand your network in a targeted manner away from the office lounge.

- **Networking in crowds**: Anyone who loves large groups and quickly gets into a conversation with new people is in good hands at trade fairs and conferences. Alternatively, you can expand a network in workshops or training courses: In small groups, interaction is more manageable, and you automatically have a topic of conversation.
- **Networking from the couch**: Business topics can be discussed, and allies found via Facebook, Twitter, or Xing. This is particularly easy in Facebook groups: They are available on a wide variety of topics and are guaranteed to find like-minded people with whom you can later discuss one or the other business idea in real life over an after-work drink. Another brilliant tool that can get the ball rolling is LinkedIn. Many careers and essential professional relationships have

begun with little research and a quick private message sent through LinkedIn. It's an excellent way to broaden your horizons from the contacts you already have and seek out more like-minded people.

- **Give and take is the cardinal rule in networking**. Anyone who demands without being able to offer something in return is likely to be lost for now. Better: make contacts without obligation and see if you can help where needed. Whether directly in a conversation or later by email or via social media: With information, a contact, or an insider tip, you can make yourself popular, and at some point, you can rely on someone who wants to return the favor. It makes sense to communicate your interests and career plans - this is the only way for the network to know exactly what you are looking for.

- **The network must be in place before it is even needed**. If you are looking for a job at the last minute through someone you have just met, you will not get a hit. Networking only pays off if you have built it up early enough and followed the rules of giving and taking. You should also analyze your network repeatedly: What are the main focuses, where is someone still missing? Here, specific contacts can be made, and the web can be expanded in a meaningful way.

- **Important: Quality comes before quantity**. This is the only way to stay in touch with your contacts and help each other out. Instead of chasing down as many business cards as possible, the targeted search for one or two contacts per event pays off more. Especially if you want to integrate people into your network in the long term, it is worth looking for people who also suit you personally and appear likable.

- **Stay updated by leveraging your online presence.** Keeping your online resume updated is an excellent way to keep your connections alive, as well as attract new ones. Recruiters can stumble on your profile just by chance. A potential contact may find your page through a mutual contact. There are so many explanations, but the fact stands that social media is a great socializing tool to put yourself out there and start a meaningful relationship with someone who can help you out.

FINALLY, A SALARY THAT SUITS ME

Men still demand higher salaries than women and prefer to negotiate. Charm and modesty are adornments but do not help you in salary negotiations: Here, it is essential to stand up for your value and pay. We will show you how women overcome internal and external resistance and get more out of salary negotiations. Downplaying your value as an employee allows companies to take advantage of you, especially if you are fully qualified to be earning as much as the males in your position. A gender pay gap exists, and part of the reason is that women are less likely to negotiate their salary when offered a job.

How to start negotiating your salary:

- The ability to negotiate your salary depends on your job. Specific jobs tend to have fixed pay rates. This means that negotiating your salary is not on the table for this position. These roles include entry-level jobs and retail or customer service jobs, among others.
- If you are in a mid to higher-level position, compensation tends to get more competitive as you slowly make your way up the career

ladder. This is where discrepancies tend to get pretty obvious when it comes to a gender pay gap.

- Be aware of gender differences. Considering these discrepancies with gender pay is an excellent tactic to use when it comes to negotiating and countering offers. Play it smart and play it cool when it comes to asking your employer for better pay.

- Let the work you have done speak for itself. Quantify your accomplishments and be assertive as you can prove your competency and ability to perform in this role that warrants a salary raise truly. Take an analytical look at all of your accomplishments, and be sure to employ them as you make your case to your boss. This is where all of your efforts accumulate as they attempt to come together and form a decisive decision on whether you deserve a raise or not.

- Show improvement. Showing that you are making a note of the feedback that is being left and using it to improve your performance even further indicates that you are valuable. You continue to be advantageous because you are always improving yourself to suit the needs of the company.

- Stop apologizing. This goes for women in any aspect of their professional life, whether about asking for a raise or a colleague's favor. Apologizing only puts a target on your back and tells people that you are meek and a pushover. Prefacing things with "I'm so sorry to bother you" "or "I feel bad asking this" takes power away from your words and removes the intent out of apologizing when you do it too many times.

- Be diplomatic. No matter what the outcome is, maintain your professionalism and keep yourself contained. If you have been rejected, the best way is to take this as a learning experience that you can consider the next time you think it is opportune to ask for a raise.

TOO NICE FOR THE JOB?

For too long, loudness has been equated with self-confidence and assertiveness. Studies show that young employees, graduates, and young professionals have long since stopped feeling like bosses who sometimes get loud when things do not go as they want. In the meantime, empathy and sympathy are the criteria that make a good manager - and that women are often ascribed to based on their gender.

So, everything is okay? Yes and no. Even those who are quiet, friendly, and nice must know what they - or she - want. Otherwise, the team will run in a direction that will not help anyone. So, while the days of roaring bosses are over and cooperation on equal terms is on the agenda, people are still needed who have a vision of where the journey should go - and who says that it must be a man? Women can do the same.

CAREER AND CHILD TOGETHER – IS THIS POSSIBLE?

This is the age-old question that plagues women around the world. Having a career and a child seems like water and oil, and many industries treat it as such. Women who are invested in their careers but manage to run a family are often told that they "have it all," which cannot be farther from the truth. Having a work-life balance is difficult when you are a full-time employee, but adding motherhood into the mix only complicates things. If you thought you didn't have time before, wait until you have kids.

The fact is that women are always sacrificing themselves to be at multiple places at once. This means missing out on certain things at each end of the spectrum. Working for long hours at work and then coming home to care for children is beyond exhausting and a Herculean task for most.

The time-out on parental leave does not necessarily have to mean the end of a woman's career - provided she take care of it. Even if it is nice to accompany the new life, thoughts about the office should find space. In the first few months of parental leave, the contact is still maintained, but after six months at the latest, women must work hard to stay on the ball professionally.

That works: With weekly meetings, part-time employment in addition to parental leave or telephone conferences in which women can keep up to date with the current state of affairs. After the baby break, many women return to part-time jobs - and thus miss another career opportunity. Presentism is still firmly anchored in many offices: those who are not physically sitting on their office armchair are de facto absent.

It is advisable to take on self-sufficient projects that are regularly presented and discussed. They can often be allocated more flexibly in terms of time and show the employer that there is still enough strength for the job - and the will to do that little bit extra for the company.

In the long term, the compatibility of work and private life is an issue that affects both genders, even if many employers still see it intensely on the part of the mothers. Fathers, who take care of a child break themselves and then share the care obligations, are generous support - and women must also actively demand them.

WHAT WOMEN WHO MADE IT SAY

Young female founders know how it has done: They have created companies out of nothing successfully in the market. In an interview with the German Huffington Post, they advise women who want to pursue a career, among other things, to strengthen networking and employ mentors - and explain why it is sometimes better for your job if you do not even know what you are getting yourself into.

Tijen O from the Women network advises women to make themselves visible and work on a self-marketing strategy that clarifies what they stand for. Whether via your blog, via social media, or in networks such as Xing or LinkedIn, anyone who establishes themselves as an expert on a topic automatically has an excellent professional standing.

Güncem C advises women to approach career planning strategically. "The job depends on other things than just hard work," says the superwoman. Endless overtime does not get anyone any further - networking skills and soft skills such as empathy and listening are much more critical. Güncem advises every woman to listen to herself: What are her strengths and weaknesses? On this basis, she should find a mentor to work with her on her development. "That would certainly have helped me in the first few years. That's why I like to support young women in their jobs."

Ida T is one of the few women who have ventured into the health tech industry. She wants to break down gender biases in the startup industry and pave the way for other women to get there. "No woman should ever hesitate to ask for help. Only if we support each other in our endeavors will women become stronger and will assert themselves - regardless of the industry, "says Ida. The ideas or yourself do not have to be perfect. The main thing is to start. "Not knowing what you're getting into at the beginning of your career is a great gift."

Christina B and her husband founded the Shiftschool in 2016, Germany's first academy for digital transformation. For them, the essential prerequisite for a successful career is the ability to take on responsibility in the job and work through topics from A to Z. "It is precious when the boss can rely on employees who are responsible for something to make decisions themselves and to stand by them. Then the boss can delegate with a clear conscience," says Christina. But it is also essential for a career to learn to believe in yourself and to trust yourself. Reflecting on the challenges you have already mastered in your life gives you strength. "Tell yourself: I can do this; I've already done completely different things."

Antonia A developed the Careship company and her brother and said: Women must not allow themselves to be dissuaded from their path and dreams - and not from anyone. "The eagerness to jump into the deep end, and also to take risks and to work with incomplete information has brought me a long way in my career." In her opinion, women should trust themselves more and learn to sell themselves well.

RESPONDING TO PEOPLE WHO SAY YOU CANNOT MAKE IT AS A WOMAN

Being a woman comes with great responsibility and, at some point - more significant setbacks. This is more so if you are a young woman. In the workplace, in any industry, at home, with peers, women find themselves in situations where others question their capabilities just because they are women. 4 out of 5 women receive sexist and offensive remarks.

You will come across people bothered by your gender or your greatness as you start working at any point in life. But do not cower in dismay because you can do something about it. Read on to find out how.

Keep Your Composure

First things first, as a young adult on the first day of work, keep your composure. Do not feel intimidated by the people at work and their insignificant opinions, and do not let it consume you. That is just what it is - a mere opinion. Reacting emotionally or defensively can only exacerbate the situation. Do not attach bearing to words that come from strangers and rude strangers at that.

Furthermore, do not attach these opinions to your competency or value as an individual. The important thing is to differentiate between constructive criticism and criticism that is entirely unwarranted and unnecessary. Doing so will set you up for success because constructive criticism can help you improve and evolve as an individual, employee, and team player.

But when it comes to people who are only looking to pass judgments about you, understand where they are coming from and remember that it is a place of insecurity from seeing a woman thrive and succeed where they were not able to. Many charlatans will underestimate your abilities. But that is just a projection of what they are – intimidated by how far you can come and how much you can achieve. Filter the words you listen to, the ones you allow to influence how you think and what you do.

Know the Motive

You can think of a way to respond when you know

your detractor's motive behind the denigration. Yes, it is ironic, but a way to understand how to respond better is understanding why. Negative criticisms are projections of an underlying inferiority complex.

It says more about the person than about you. They may feel threatened by your power, or they are not willing to learn under you. They also want to be at par with you, but they know they just cannot. Shame with a hint of anger may have also prompted the affront.

Understanding their motives can help you reconfigure their words to be far less hurtful because, ultimately, we are human beings with feelings. You will feel attacked, and the urge to get defensive will make itself known. But the fact is, knowing that their attacks come from their underlying insecurities helps you see that the fault does not indeed lie within yourself.

Retaliate when Ready

There is nothing wrong with retaliating, especially if you are the affected one. However, not all vilifiers warrant your response. You need not explain. If they only want to shake your confidence and have nothing worthwhile to spend their time on, better not invest yours in getting back at them.

Silence is an act of better revenge. It takes a sheer amount of courage and conviction to counter your critic's disapproval. But you do not always have to. It is a way to get the message across that you are a woman of purpose whose time you invest only in your commitments and the things that matter. Better let your success be your indignant statement.

Call them out and Discourse

When men's affront are out of bounds, pull them up on their sexism and engage them in a conversation. Make them realize that gender is not a measure of competence. See, many women are now on the rise, and in fact, some are in leadership positions. It is a golden reason to take pride in your being. Being a woman is not a mistake. It is a strength, so do not apologize nor explain. Your identity as a woman is your answer.

When others denigrate you just because you are a woman, mostly young, keep your calm and collect your thoughts. Never stoop down to their level. Show them that gender is not a measure of competence, and success knows no sex. In-home life and the work-place, women are the masters of commitment, so there is absolutely no reason for the belittling.

11 CAREER TIPS WITH GUARANTEED SUCCESS

✔ **More courage with applications**: It is perfectly okay to apply for job advertisements whose requirements are only met by 60-70%.

✔ **Enter the competition**: It does not always have to be faster, higher, and further: Smart solutions often lead to more than sheer muscle power.

✔ **Appreciate your performance**: What you have achieved is worth a lot - you can be proud and build on it.

✔ **Mathematics, science, and sport**: women can do everything they want, even if clichés often suggest the opposite.

✔ **Make financial demands**: no woman must be satisfied with what she has.

✔ **Negotiating**: Whether salary or area of responsibility: You can learn to negotiate - and sometimes it is even fun.

✓ **Pushing for promotion**: If it does not work the first time, stick with it: A follow-up interview a few months later often brings the desired result.

✓ **Support bosses**: For networks function, prejudices must get support from the head and women in their team's management positions.

✓ **Get the best of both worlds**: "Male" characteristics such as power-conscious, assertive, and self-confident work wonders in conjunction with "female" attributes such as communicative, diplomatic, and sensitive.

✓ **Look for a managerial position**: should someone else look after the household and children. Women are now making a career.

✓ **Praise yourself**: Nobody gets bored talking about their strengths

SIX TIPS ON HOW YOU CAN MAKE A CAREER AS A YOUNG WOMAN

Career advancement is not only reserved for men. The tips reveal how you can make a career as a young woman.

There are many career planning guides out there that cater to both men and women. But women who wish to make a career should avoid a few pitfalls so that the way up does not end in a dead-end. But how can you successfully circumnavigate these cliffs? Here are six tips that should help you to develop a career as a woman.

Tip 1 - do not present yourself as a glamorous girl!

Do not fight with the woman's arms! You are not there to seduce your boss; instead, you plan to take his post someday. Even if you have a flawless figure: mini-skirt and deep necklines do not belong in the workplace.

Better this way: Wear costumes and combine them with colored tops and scarves. Go to the hairdresser and apply make-up discreetly. You are a woman, after all!

The counterpart to the glamour girl, the hard-working grey mouse who hopes that her performance will be noticed and rewarded, but is practically invisible, will not have a career.

Ultimately, being comfortable in your skin brings about the confidence that simply cannot be replicated.

So, while it is important to dress professionally and appropriately, that does not mean that you cannot have a personality.

Tip 2 - Present your work confidently

Women tend to view humility as the highest virtue. That is counterproductive in professional life! Do not make yourself smaller than you are! Once you start, after graduation, flaunt your accomplishments to decision-makers.

Your work is an extension of you. You want your efforts to go noticed because they attest to your abilities and competencies. By presenting your work confidently, you signify to everyone in the room that you want their attention on the work you have done. Being meek only leads people to think that your appointment is not up to par and is not worth spending time on.

When you are praised, take it for granted. For example, answer: "Yes, I got the project off well; there is a lot of work behind it." You may then immediately follow up with a question about promotion or a salary increase.

Tip 3 - Use your social skills but do it properly!

If you want to make a career as a young woman, you have something decisive ahead of men, namely higher social skills. Because women are more communicative, they can grasp moods in individuals or groups more quickly and react appropriately. Therefore, the participation of women in disputes has a balancing effect because their contributions contain compromises, which leads to more constructive results than if the men attack each other like gamecocks.

The other side of the coin: Don't become the department's suggestion box for sheer empathy. Also, do not accept that your colleague will pass work onto you because of lovesickness. Postpone private calls to breaks and after work!

Tip 4 – Contribute to meetings

On no occasion do men and women behave as obviously different as they do in business meetings. Not only do men speak up significantly more often, but they also do so with self-confidence that often cannot be objectively justified. If you want to make a career as a woman, you must catch up with men on this point. So, hands up and speak out before your colleague does! It is best to have an introductory sentence ready if it is your turn. And not "I would think" or "maybe it could be that" (typically feminine formulations) but "I believe," "the fact is," or "it is clear that."

Tip 5 - the "family trap."

That is the most delicate point. When applying, women, unlike men, are often asked whether they are planning to start a family. If you want to have a career as a woman, you must clarify that work has a top priority. Better to avoid words like "part-time" or "back off." Then, when there is indeed a baby, you will not need to be feeling guilty. You are not a bad mother if your child is well looked after, including by you, but not around the clock.

Tip 6 - learn to talk

Did you do a good job? Then stand by it and show it with exact words. Anyone who wants to fill a management position must be able to give good speeches. This is the only way to convince. Having strong public speaking capabilities can set you apart in a room full of noise. Not only are you far more eloquent and well-thought-out, but you also come off well-prepared and knowledgeable. Remember, leaving a lasting impression can assert your role in the room and beyond.

HOW TO DEAL WITH DISCRIMINATION AT THE WORKPLACE FOR WOMEN

Society favors you if you are not a woman. A challenging, cold, dismaying fact that exists in the workplace today. Discrimination against women may come in all forms - being paid relatively less, harassed by words and action, or denying the opportunity or promotion they deserve.

If you are a woman with such experience, rise from that place of silence that only benefits your oppressors. But first, you need to know when an act or a remark is a sign of discrimination.

Equalrights.org outlines the many forms of discrimination with legal bearing and could earn the perpetrators a one-way ticket to court. Discrimination includes the following.

- Denied a position in the workplace because of your gender
- Receiving a lower salary compared to male counterparts

- Being evaluated on a more stringent standard
  or criteria
- Penalized for not conforming to standards
- Refrained from opportunities like training,
  promotion, or a pay raise
- Forced to pick up the slack or quit because
  you are young and a woman
- You are being insulted and called derogatory
  slurs and names.

Courage will breed from knowledge. It perceives
when it is time to stand up and how it is crucial. Read
on to know what else you can do once you find yourself on the receiving end of assault or prejudice.

Know Your Rights

- It is your right to work in a fair and safe
  space and an environment free from
  discrimination.
- You can express your thoughts on
  discrimination and your intentions to foster a
  safe, discrimination-free environment for you
  and your colleagues. You can pull people
  into the conversation and eventually mitigate
  such a pressing issue. Know that it is illegal

for the employer to penalize you for
doing so.

- It is your right to report to your immediate
superiors or the human resource personnel
about any form of harassment you
experience at work.

- If your employer reduces or withholds your
salary, fires you from work, or demotes you
for doing these things, you can sue under
these grounds. Note that any form of
retaliation from your employer is illegal.

Document Your Experience

On the onset, write every experience, every word, or
action done in an assault. It may not be as easy as it
sounds, but this will help support your complaints
later. Keep them objective and factual as much as
possible. Keep records of messages, e-mails, or
pictures for you to use when needed. Pen down the
names of witnesses and their contact numbers. When
your employer retaliates at you, record every detail
and keep them in a place or electronic storage where
only you or people you trust can access.

Review Policies of the Workplace

Look for the companies' policies regarding discrimination. Study the procedures you need to undergo if you experience the same, the necessary steps to take when raising a complaint, and the people you need to consult with your concern. Keep a record of their contact numbers and requirements in case the need arises.

Report to Your Higher-ups

Armed with the knowledge of the complaint procedures, you can report your situation to your boss, or your HR. Equalrights.org suggests that you commit your complaint into writing, whether by letter or e-mail and keep several copies for proof. When you face discrimination as a woman, do not let their intimidation or your fear silence you. Deal with it head-on and take action as mentioned above. Always be on guard and keep track of your experience. Women, especially fresh grads and young adults, must hold their ground and stand up until the workplace completely eradicates discrimination and leaves no room for double standards

CAREER ADVICE FOR GRADUATES: WHAT SHOULD I BE?

---

*W*hich job is right for me?

Many young people ask themselves this question after completing their studies and training. They are often overwhelmed by the numerous training opportunities, fields of study, job profiles, and their environment's expectations. For fear of a wrong decision, either none is made at all, or they choose the path that their parents have planned for them.

This is a terrifying time because the pressure to have absolutely every detail mapped out is hugely stressful for young people. The question itself is often brought up in interviews: "Where do you see yourself in five years?" Can most people honestly answer that question fully? The answer is no, and most people do not have a fully fleshed-out plan that defines their trajectory for the next five years of their life. Many have a general idea. There is no denying that. But the fact still stands that the expectation is doubled for recent graduates. For young people, this becomes an expectation in and of itself the minute they graduate. The next steps, ambitions, and plans have to be completely figured out to move on from being a student and into the next stage of their lives, which is now a workforce member.

Am I striving for recognition, power, or independence? Does competition or status motivate me? Am I a team, squad player, or a loner? And: who are my role models? Who can I learn from? Who can support me in deciding on a career? These questions are essential when looking for the right job.

We have the answers in this book, and it will help you in intensive one-on-one conversations

- recognize your skills, needs, and values,
- to strengthen trust in you,
- find out which life motives and family characteristics are essential and useful for your professional life,

- develop a concrete plan - with clear and individual strategies for your career choice.

CAREER ENTRY AFTER GRADUATION

After graduating from university, there are various options for taking up a job. Preparing early and looking for a job makes the transition from studying to work easier.

When you have graduated from your university, you will enter the ocean of career seekers to be a part of a dynamic work sector. One factor you must prepare yourself for is intense rivalry from other career-seekers. Because you have only come from a university and no structured job experience to render you the top pick for jobs, it might be complicated.

But do not let this rob you of your faith. Suppose you are at a point where you are always learning to improve your abilities in the industry. There are strategies to become highly employable even though you are a recent graduate. Consider these strategies to take advantage of and outperform other existing professionals.

Training Program

HR departments, government agencies, and recruiting companies embrace emerging technology, including the usage of job-hunting sites and LinkedIn or Facebook Jobs, for posting training programs.

Take time to visit these pages to see what sites publish further work openings or which businesses have earned constructive input from career-seekers. Then build profiles on your preferred worksites and provide your full profile.

Now you should start partaking in the program, completing it, and finally searching for work, based on employers ready to hire new graduates.

Internship

You might run across employers that favor seasoned applicants over young graduates to gain unique skillsets that can only be established over time.

To support you get out of these skills shortages, you should grab the opportunity of the community's internship or volunteering programs. These workshops may offer valuable exposure and experience in critical fields, namely, project management or skills enhancement.

Often, even though they plan to recruit you formally in their company, they will act as a kick-starter to launch your career.

Direct Entry

Your first work prospect does not need to originate from a fair profession. You can prefer to be cautious about seeking a job or employer when you take advantage of your contacts, such as relatives, colleagues, advisors, and those who may be willing to recommend you to possible recruiters or organizations.

Let the people on your network realize that you are searching for career openings. Alternatively, you may want to study businesses where you want to work, as well as notifying your social media friends to inquire about job opportunities in a similar industry.

You will also have to venture through the correct channels to submit, but your edge has already had some favorable opportunities.

Feeling demotivated? Here is how you can handle it

Do not forget what constructive thoughts will bring for your work search efforts. The change from a university existence to a productive hardworking person may render you feeling drained, demotivated, or challenged.

Although this feeling is legitimate, you must remain centered on your job goals— read insightful blogs and books, refresh your website, practice answering typical questions, and more. The plan here is to create a concrete plan for everything that you will do.

Landing the first career opportunity is not as daunting as you believe it is. Take advantage of these tools to help you become as successful as any other applicant in the industry, regardless of the degree of expertise.

Once you have landed your first career opportunity, it is also important to remember that even though your first job may not be your first choice, it certainly does not define your career for the rest of your life. First jobs are a great stepping-stone to the career path you genuinely aspire for, even if the work seems to not align with your ambitions. The vital thing to remember or bear in mind here is that it is a relevant experience, which is tremendously valued as job markets grow increasingly competitive.

Rather than looking at your first job or internship critically, look at it from the lens of what practical skills you can learn and take to your next appointment. Too often do young people get extremely disheartened because they are in a role that they were not necessarily gunning for. But the experience, especially one relevant to the field you are interested in, is crucial for a young person. Showing diverse work history and an advanced skill set can bring you even more opportunities as you choose to advance in your career.

Good luck with your potential career!

JOB QUALIFICATION PROGRAMS

Job qualification programs are vocational certificates for fresh university graduates, also an aspect of the success in landing a job in an industry. They are typically related to a specific sector and are structured to strengthen and acquire the necessary skills for your career route.

Benefits of Qualification Programs

Through qualification programs, you will gain the following benefits:

- Eligibility to work
- Strengthening your CV
- Gaining professional status
- Learning new skillsets
- Promotion

How to Find Qualification Programs

To become qualified in your preferred occupation, you must first find a suitable industry. Then, you would often go through a process to fulfill a technical qualification. For example, whether you wish to be a certified accountant or engineer.

Typically, if you choose to be a part of a formal association or institution, you will still need to be certified. As a consequence, the bulk of technical certificates are approved by professional entities.

For instance, several graduates who wish to become certified accountants would prepare for an Institute of Chartered Accountants in England and Wales or ICAEW certification.

Things to Consider When Looking for the Right Program

Most industries have some form of industry-specific certifications or technical qualifications, so selecting a related industry is essential. It is not about the regular suspects, namely judges, surgeons, and attorneys, who train for professional licensures. For instance, you can receive specialist certificates in fields such as advertisement, sales, banking, and sport.

Additionally, you should also consider the time of completion. It may take a couple of weeks and a few years to acquire such technical credentials. Flexibility is also the secret to accomplishing a technical course since most career pursuers study while employed full-time. So, many technical classes are either part-time or delivered by distance learning.

Look for the skillsets that you need to learn in a job qualification program. Most of the main graduation plans, school leavers services, and training programs require their interns to strive for a distinct technical degree while at the same time obtaining on-the-job immersion.

While entry-level programs are usually free for fresh graduates, any specialist credentials can be costly, just like the LPC. Probably, you are going to have to find out whether it is a wise expenditure or not. However, the employer may be in a role to support or contribute to the bill. For example, in hindsight, individual law firms would pay the LPC's expense for any trainees they take on.

The level of commitment is also one of those things that you need to consider. You would still need to decide whether it is worth spending time and dedication to gain a technical certification or not. Is it going to improve your career? Is it going to get you additional attention or increase your salary? Many students waste money on the acquisition of a technical degree before they even get a promising job.

When enrolling in a technical qualification course, verify that the certification you earn is related to your career, and confirm that a professional entity exists. The main thing to note is that a well-chosen technical certificate could boost your chances of getting employed amongst all other benefits.

HOW TO PREPARE FOR YOUR FUTURE JOB AS A STUDENT

Preparing for your future job as a student is crucial. It is a better investment of your time than throwing parties and getting distracted. There is nothing wrong with having fun but remember that the real world has high expectations for the new workforce. As early as you can, build your resume. You can also try these tips to be a valuable asset in your future company.

Choice of specializations

Choose the career that you do not mind doing for decades. Let it be something that aligns with your interests and lucrative enough to sustain your needs. In making this decision, you need self-awareness and knowledge of your desired career to guide you. Pick the specialization that suits your aptitudes and skills lest you dread your work each time. Set realistic expectations and work on the skills you need for the job.

Voluntary study internships

You can do your research about the career paths you are interested in. You can read about them, but nothing beats a hands-on learning experience. Sign up for internships when you can. This will give you a glimpse of the heart of the work. You learn the essentials, the basics in and out of your specialization. You get training and advice from people who have worked for years. You can start with a small business within your community and help them grow.

Project work

Embark on a project you choose for yourself. While you are at it, allow yourself to make mistakes. This is just one of the meaningful ways to learn. The more blunders you make, the better you become at your craft. This is one answer to how you can prepare yourself in the future. Remember that it is a rat race out there in the world. Experience is your armor.

Thesis topic

Another thing you can add to your knowledge is completing a thesis that interests you and you believe is impactful. Choose a thesis topic that reflects your passion so you do not have a hard time writing it. This hones your research skills and your initiative to get the work done. In short, remember these three things 1) list the topics that interest you, 2) sort the issue that you care about researching, and 3) choose the best case that also relates to your chosen specialization.

Part-time employment

You can also search for part-time jobs if you wish to make extra money while gaining experience. Aside from the extra bucks, you acquire the following skills.

- *Time Management*. This is the most given skill you can gain by landing a part-time job. You master how to balance your responsibilities as a student and an employee.
- *Independence*. You learn the right work ethics even under pressure.
- *Financial management skills*. As you are earning, you learn how to manage your money and set aside your expenses and savings.
- *Interpersonal skills*. When you are out there, you are bound to meet people and communicate with them, especially if you are in a place where you provide value to clients or customers.
- *Professional network*. This is a place where you can at least start to build professional connections too. They will be valuable to you as you journey through your work life and post studies.

Voluntary work

Engage with your community and extend your relevant talents. This is also one way to make connections and build meaningful relationships. You can meet people and learn from their experiences related to your career choice. You gain knowledge, hone practical skills, and make an impact at the same time. It is also a bonus for your resume. Learning has no limits, and the ones you gain from hands-on experience equip you better.

Foreign language skills

Communication and public speaking are soft skills you can learn if you commit to them. Learning a foreign language is especially relevant to you if you plan to work abroad. There are apps and free online resources that you can access to aid your learning. Know the country's culture and research information about it in advance, so you do not get lost - literally and figuratively, later.

Specific IT skills

Technology has shaped the systems of the workplace. This is better to be on your list of skills to learn. From the most basic, like writing emails to learning about programming and other software, you can start somewhere. You need not be a master of all; you just need to put in the work and learn the fundamentals.

As a learner, there are a lot of options for you to gain experience and develop your skills. Follow the steps above and leave the room for growth open. Keep your willingness to improve. It will not be too easy, but it will be worth it. You will reap the rewards for the efforts you have put in.

JOB HUNTING TIPS FOR GRADUATES

Being able to get out of college with a hard-fought degree can be very liberating. No more all-nighters, no more crammed reviewing for exams, etc. Though it may seem like you have figured out everything, graduating from college is just a single step towards the real world.

As a graduate, you will be met with responsibilities and obligations like supporting your family or providing food on the table. All these things will only be possible when you land a job. However, this begs the question, "how do I land a job?" Well, here are job hunting tips for graduates like you to consider!

Resumes and Cover Letters

Your degree will likely determine the job you would apply for since it will suit your qualification. Regardless of what you graduate with, whether Latin honors or not, accept that people will most likely not recognize you. That is why you will need to introduce yourself to them first, hence the need for resumes and cover letters.

Resumes are to be understandable and straightforward, but they must capture who you are. HR professionals do not dwell on technical details, so keep it away from jargons. Additionally, highlight the actual contents like your achievements, expertise, and extracurricular activities relevant to the job description.

Cover letters must also follow suit. Begin with introducing yourself and then dwell on your motivation in applying for the job. You must even convince them about why they should hire you, so make sure to mention why you are the perfect person for the job.

Moreover, tell them what you can contribute to their company once you have been hired.

Unsolicited Applications

These applications are a bit different from the previously discussed. There are instances when you take an interest in applying for a job, but there might not be an opening or hiring for an exciting position at the moment. You can still send a letter of application, but it is referred to as an unsolicited one.

The main difference is that this application requires more intensive research on the company or the position. You must be familiar with the employer or the work culture and express sincerity as to why you want to participate in the job. Like solicited applications (has announced job openings), you again must mention how you can be an asset to them.

Declined Applications

Application denials can occur even without the interview taking place yet. When these instances happen, it can be for one of two reasons: there is someone more suitable, or your resume was the problem.

When you continuously apply for work yet get consistent rejections, check your resume and identify what is wrong. It might lack substance. Every application letter must be unique to each company. Keep it short and sweet but make sure to capture them with the carefully selected words you will use.

Interviews

Make an impression. From your attire to the way you answer questions, to the contents of your answer, will determine whether you will get the job or not. Remember that being in an interview means that you can resume work or have an on-paper qualification that has worked. They just need to know you and what you can do.

Plan out what you will be wearing for the interview— something presentable, which will make you feel confident. Plan out your consultation by answering common job interview questions. Create concrete answers in your head. This way, when you sit in front of the recruiter, you will grasp what to say.

First Day

Your first day, ah yes, finally it has arrived. It is not a competition. You do not have to make your boss coffee and clean the bathroom altogether to impress them. You just must do the job description and fulfill what you have promised to offer them during your application.

Ask relevant job questions; this shows curiosity and investment in the job. Prepare to answer questions from colleagues who are asking you about yourself and your previous employments. Everything will be okay. Just smile, relax, familiarize yourself with the work dynamics, and make friends. You will adapt there soon enough.

WHERE TO GET SUPPORT?

Leaping from being a university student to being an employee who must face real-life challenges might be scary at first. Therefore, you need support from experts and the people who genuinely care about you to make this transition as smooth as possible. Here are some places and people you can seek help from in making your transition from being a student to being an employee.

Special literature

This unique literature involves research and articles formulated focusing on a specific topic, and in this case, employment and job opportunities. Do your research and look closely into these kinds of literature. These scholarly articles will provide you with the facts and information like statistics and different studies to help you transition.

Internet

You can also take advantage of the golden era of technology by using the internet and researching various ways on how you can make the transition from being a student to being an employee in a smooth manner. There are countless blogs, podcasts, videos, and tutorials on how you can do this. All you are expected to do is to be resourceful and fact-check your research first before anything else.

Job consultations

Another thing you can do is to seek the help of a consultant. These job consultations aim to answer your questions about making the transition from "student life" to "real life." The viewpoints and opinions you will be hearing will be coming from the experts in the field so you can be sure that it is reliable and accurate.

Mentors

Having a mentor to guide you through anything is one of the best things you can have. Your mentor might be an expert in the field or even just someone who has any experiences that they can relay to you, which in turn can help make your transition smooth and easy. Your mentor might be a close friend who has enough experience or your former professors in school.

Family

Lastly, you can turn to the people who would not charge you fees for their advice and who would provide you with all the love and support they can give as you take the step to another chapter of your life - your family. You can ask your parents or your older siblings how they did it back when they were fresh graduates and were looking for a job.

The transition from being a student who is worried about passing assignments on time and joining various contests to being an employee who must face real-life challenges is hard. Still, it can be made smooth and easy if you only know where to look and seek support. Many people have already experienced what you are about to go through. You just must ask them for guidance and listen to the advice they give.

ADDITIONAL TRAINING?

To get into a job faster or more successfully, some graduates do plan additional training. However, this exclusive makes sense if it is generally required (e.g., medicine) or qualified for a specific function (e.g., high school teacher). However, for most graduates, the first step is to acquire professional experience and not even more theory.

CAREER MANAGEMENT

*C*areer management is the lifelong practice of investing resources to achieve your career goals. Career management is not one event but a continuing process necessary to adapt to the 21st Century economy's changing demands—career Vision's schedule supports ongoing personal and professional development throughout life's transitions.

Even if we are in the early phase of our work life or are workforce veterans, we have probably heard the term career management. We have likewise probably heard that in the future we need to be responsible for our careers. What we may not have n disclosed is what career management is and how we should do it! Career management uses concepts similar to sound financial management. A great rule of thumb to keep in mind is that a disciplined investment, made regularly, yields a greater return. Although the tactics will differ, career management focuses on two critical investment assets to manage throughout our working years, our lifelong personal learning and our network of relationships.

LIFELONG LEARNING

It is often startling to realize how much of our day-to-day work is now based around technology: computers and other scientific advancements, which have radically altered how we conduct our work. The consequence of these advancements and innovations will ripple very swiftly through the economy, obsolescing many businesses and catapulting others into the limelight. How well we can adapt to these ongoing innovations will directly relate to how we keep our knowledge and skills. Consider how to diversify your investments in time, energy, and resources. Examples might incorporate credentialed coursework (locally or through distance learning), topical courses for certificates, joining cutting-edge projects, attending seminars, or staying current in professional reading.

NETWORK OF RELATIONSHIPS

As we have moved to an information and service economy, relationship contacts have become an increasingly critical asset. Not only do our relationships help us accomplish our day-to-day tasks with colleagues, vendors, customers, and competitors, but these relationships will also be the source of information about how fields and industries are evolving. We also have contacts outside of our work environments affiliated with our hobbies, children, spiritual, or community networks. These personal and professional contacts will transcend specific companies, industries, and organizations. How we interact, reply, and connect in all our communications will impact our current performance and future opportunities. Very limited is accomplished in isolation. Networking uncovers more than 71% of current job openings.

Keeping connected with contacts and knowing how to build good relationships is more important than ever before. These skills can be advanced in applied communication courses, mastering contact management software, effective listening, and an honest desire to get to know people better.

Lifelong training, relationship, and contact management form the backdrop of successful career management. Starting a vision and plan are also essential for guiding informed investment decisions and establishing annual goals. The career vision we select should be broad enough to be flexible but definitive enough to be actionable. This career vision, built on a profile of our unique traits, directs our choices to develop what we need to be satisfied and be able to contribute to different work environments over the years successfully. To manage our adaptability and employability, habitually establishing annual learning objectives and nurturing our relationships are the keys to productive career management.

CAREER MANAGEMENT PROCESS

Career Management is a life-long development of investing resources to accomplish your future career goals. It is a continuing development that allows you to adapt to the changing demands of our dynamic economy. Career management development embraces various concepts: Self-awareness, career development, planning/career exploration, life-long learning, and networking.

SELF-AWARENESS

Look at yourself to reveal your interests, skills, personality traits, and values. You can start by asking yourself the questions below:

- Who are you?
- What interests you?
- What do you like to do?
- What are you good at doing?
- What do you value, what is important to you?
- What are your unique assets, skills, and abilities?
- Who requires the talents, skills, and abilities you can provide?
- What work environment and arrangements make sense to you?
- What activities do I find fun, motivating, engaging, and enjoyable?
- What skills do you need to have to develop and manage your career?

- What personal style or peculiarity do I have
  that are essential to me in the workplace?

Ask friends, colleagues, family members, co-workers,
professors, or mentors if they identify the same qualities in you as you see in yourself.

CAREER DEVELOPMENT PLANNING/CAREER EXPLORATION

Career Development Planning is a system designed to
help you:

- Take the time to reflect on your job/career
  goals
- Focus and target on developing knowledge
  and skills for your current position and future
  job opportunities
- Think about how you can utilize your
  strengths, talents, experience, and
  motivation efficiently – how can you use all
  these aspects to increase your passion for
  work!
- Be the architect of your career development
  plan – write your goals, decide to have a plan
  for your career development

- Discuss your career process goals with your manager.

Once you have made a career decision or choice, you now need to plan how you will decide. A career plan provides vision, direction, structure, and motivation for your career management process.

WHAT DO YOU THINK OF CAREER PROCESS PLANNING?

Usually, when we think of career management, we think of the goals or action items we need to move our careers forward. Often, we carry some of these thoughts around in our heads for long periods without ever writing them down. If we do pen down our goals, they usually take the form of a list, and many times we lose motivation after writing our goals down, misplace the list, and attain only some of our dreams. That is why this style of thinking and just penning your career objectives is not a very motivating or reinforcing process!

It is far more potent, motivating, and productive to think of career planning as a process that allows us to envision our future careers and then provides us with a path to pursue our goals and realize our dreams. Career planning is not something that happens once or twice in one's career. On the contrary, it is a recurring process of taking the time to assess one's identity, setting new goals, creating new career horizons, and celebrating successes as one develops and becomes more knowledgeable and skilled

Good performance, perseverance, and relationships - with this trio, you will quickly get up the career ladder. But as soon as some climb the steps - they fall just as quickly. Because on the way to the top, some stumbling blocks have messed up their careers. Indeed, mistakes can never be avoided entirely. But your risk becomes smaller when you know these typical career killers. You have already taken the leading step towards this: you are reading this book- and hopefully, you can identify the most common career killers and successfully avoid them.

YOU OBSTRUCT YOUR CAREER

Has a colleague suggested to you a promotion path? Has your career been stagnated? It would be easy now to blame the incompetent boss or the slimy colleague for your failure. But the truth is more uncomfortable: most workers stand in their way as they advance.

Technical competence is only one side of the coin. If you want to get ahead in your job, you must be highly committed, continuously develop yourself, know the game's rules, and perform specific job behaviors. Otherwise, others will pass you by.

Taking responsibility for one's actions and possibly for setbacks is certainly not always easy. You can only consciously avoid frequent career killers and shape your professional future if you take matters into your own hands.

Sometimes even the little things are enough to cause lasting harm or to land in a career impasse. Therefore, do not view the following list of errors as regulations or charges. Instead, it should serve to raise awareness of these potential career killers.

ENDING THE PROMOTION

Endless frustration.

Anyone who sneaks through the office floors with drooping heads, as if they were carrying the company's burden on their shoulders, will soon stomp in the basement. Nobody likes certified fun brakes. Especially not in times of crisis. This calls for types who spread optimism, not an apocalyptic mood.

For you, constant frustration quickly turns into a career killer. If you are always dissatisfied and believe that your career advancement will not work out anyway, it will probably be the same. You can only make a career if others believe in you - but for that to be possible, you must think that you can do it.

Product disappointment.

It is the worst thing a company can do to its customers. Customers have zero tolerance for this and never buy again. Therefore, never make promises that you cannot keep. Neither when taking on a project nor during a promotion, let alone in an interview.

In doing so, you are only fueling unrealistic and harmful expectations. The first time, the self-inflicted disappointment may not seem so bad. But with every subsequent time, it undermines trust in you. They mutate into a blender - without any external compulsion. With all understanding of self-marketing: Don't stack too high, especially at the beginning. There are many advantages to being underestimated - even if it is only that you can surprise business partners, colleagues, and bosses: positively.

Arrogance.

Young colleagues and young professionals believe that it is smart to shine through so much performance that it even puts their boss in the shade. Huge mistake! Those who let their talents shine brighter than those of the boss inevitably arouse their envy and distrust. And that ends badly.

Just watch what happens when someone optimizes the boss's idea with your own in the next meeting. Please just observe, do not try it yourself! That is why true professionals play beyond gangs - they naturally make the boss look smarter than themselves, for example, by asking them for advice. Mighty people are enthusiastic about such requests. Only a boss who has been able to give you the gift of their superiority will protect you permanently.

Advice resistance.

Of course, not every colleague who gives you advice means well. Sometimes it is intrigue, or a wrong track, or an attempt to make yourself bigger as an advisor. However, these are rather exceptions. As a rule, the help you need now can only be found one office away. And it would be stupid not to take advantage of this opportunity.

It is even more stupid not to learn from people who may be further than you and have more experience. Anyone who thinks that this is how they document their independence is making a grave mistake: they remain dependent on their competence and creativity. And that is just not always enough. Often it is only pride that keeps us from doing it - and therefore keeps us small.

If you ask for tips or help, you may feel small at first. In the long run, however, it will surpass itself. And on top of that, it builds a valuable network of advisors and mentors.

False modesty

Modesty is an ornament - you get no further without it: As vain and unpleasant as self-portrayal may seem, whoever does not attract attention falls through the grid. Even the most outstanding achievement fizzles out if nobody notices it. This constant advertising naturally requires a sure instinct; otherwise, it quickly drifts into self-importance.

In your job, you should be wiser. Tried and tested methods provide regular interim reports and progress reports for larger tasks, for example. Or speak up in meetings. Not all the time, but with well-developed, fresh ideas. Or you offer your knowledge and help to other colleagues. This has the advantage that they will talk positively about you later. And word of mouth is even more effective than self-promotion.

Perfectionism.

It is a mistake not to want to make mistakes. Some individuals waste their whole lives trying to do this. Objectively speaking, they may be less likely to make mistakes than others. But they also do less because they spend a lot of time avoiding potential errors. Of course, it is wise to set high standards for yourself and others. But only if they are realistic.

Otherwise, perfectionism will only hold you back. It leads to tunnel vision in which those affected concentrate on details that are of little importance for the big picture. Defects can broaden one's horizons: Without mistakes, Christopher Columbus would never have discovered America. Successful people are characterized precisely by the fact that they make mistakes because they do more than others. An error is not bad if it is not repeated, and you learn from it.

Like the IBM founder Tom Watson, when one of his employees made a severe mistake, it cost him $ 600,000. Watson was then asked if he would fire the employee, which Watson vehemently denied. He just said, I just invested $ 600,000 in his education. Why would anyone else get this experience for free? Note: only gods can afford zero tolerance for errors.

Loquacity.

The cabaret artist Willy Reichert once said: Gossip is the tangible connection between two loose tongues. Many people immediately believe what is whispered. Indiscretion often spreads faster than noise. Insidious!

It is not uncommon for the short-term feeling of superiority to proclaim something that no one knows yet as a Pyrrhic victory. First, because some of the dirt always sticks to the thrower. Second, because blasphemy does not exactly indicate a noble character. Third, because communication may turn out to be untrue, then the author is either considered a liar or an unsuspecting pomposity. Both are bad.

There is hardly anything that damages the career as much as the image of a localized leak. King Solomon warned his pupils: Anyone who acts as gossip is divulging secrets. So, do not get involved with someone who talks a lot.

Stubbornness.

Every company has its own culture. Behind it are often unwritten rules for dealing with one another, for procedures in meetings, language codes, or reporting chains. It is good not to leave the office before 7 p.m. Others always take their department for lunch or hand out coffee and cake on their birthday.

Still, others see poor elbow use as a sign of weakness. No matter how much you insist on your individuality: Playing along is a must. Or they'd better look for a different team and company. Such behavior patterns are always also a kind of immunity test: Those who cannot assimilate into the organism will soon be rejected.

Job starters do well to find out quickly which rules are being played and worked by. The best strategy for the first few weeks: listens carefully, watch - and shut up.

Self-doubt. (Permanent)

If you are one of those people who weigh everything carefully before starting, who always check all the details and still find a fly in the ointment in the end, then you should read this point particularly carefully. Everyone knows the phrase If only I ... then ...! If only I had more responsibility, I could achieve more. If I had more power, things would change here. If I had more money, I would be happier.

Such doubts are underhanded. If you think pessimistically, you usually have a distorted perception. Notorious pessimists are no longer able to look at problems from a neutral position from a sufficient distance. Result: You can only see the mountain and no longer the summit. Quite a few then stop in front of the obstacle, turn around, or prefer to take countless, supposedly easier detours. Do not let the conditions chase you down!

You can also reach the summit in stages. Think about where you are and what needs to be done next to get one step closer to that goal. And then go ahead. Step by step. Base camp for base camp. If you have never achieved anything, let us go, guys, and achieve everything.

Impatience.

Impatience is a weakness - a big one. I want! Everything! Now! Attitude only creates instant types who desire too fast and too much at once but are not (yet) up to the task (see also overconfidence). You cannot have three years of experience in one. It is the practice that makes perfect.

It takes patience to manage a challenging project and even more so to lead other people. But being able to wait can even be a virtue. Some problems can be solved by themselves, or over time you will receive information and ideas that enable a better solution. The express elevator to a career is and will remain a myth.

There is much more strength in rest. Plus, nothing is more frustrating than climbing the corporate ladder at a rapid pace only to find out at the top that you have laid it on the wrong wall.

Ingratitude

Even geniuses sometimes need the help of others. Be it that they provide you with useful information, warn you in good time, or actively protect you. The more mentors you have, the better. A functioning network of relationships and lots of B vitamins act as a career turbo.

But it can also quickly become a career killer if you forget about your contacts. And it is effortless: Simply forget who was at your side with advice and action and from whom you have benefited in some form so far. No one expects immediate consideration for such favors. Only those who forget this guilt are engaged in self-sabotage of the first order.

Goethe already considered ingratitude to be a weakness: I have never seen capable people being ungrateful. Ingratitude is not a trivial offense but a gross violation of a professional iron law: one hand washes the other.

Aimlessness

That, too, is an iron law of success: strong personalities do not hang around. If you want to give wings to your career, you have to make consistent decisions -

also on your behalf. To do this, however, you first must know exactly what you want. This is the only way to gain clarity in your head and tenacity in action.

Indeed, there are always overly committed people who do not turn down a request and manage several projects simultaneously - but they do not get any further. You have more stress and less fun. If you tackle everything somehow, you do not do anything well. Top performance, on the other hand, only arises when you fully concentrate on a specific goal. There-fore, everyone should (and again and again) ask themselves:

- What exactly do I want to achieve?
- What should change or improve in my life?
- Why is this goal so important to me?
- What must be done to achieve it?
- What can I do?
- Is that enough for that?
- What would I have to do without?

Such goals are welcome to change. After all, clinging to a plan forever or staying too long in a job can also be an expression of aimlessness. The main thing is that you remain aware of it and keep moving. Because it is still like this: a career is not a coincidence - it is made.

As a soon-to-be university grad, I know that the world of work can catch you unaware. In preparing for the job search, I have found that experienced professionals often have great advice to dispense (also some not-so-great advice, but that is a topic for another book).

And, indeed, sometimes the wisest tips do not come from experts but real people with real and true stories. With that in mind, The Muse team requested the LinkedIn community what wisdom they would bestow on recent grads.

More students are eager to work with university certificates, with the yearly competition.

Are you looking for job advice for recent graduates?

If you experience any of these fears:

- You are eager to put your new college degree to use but do not have your perfect job lined up.

- You are worried that you may have a lack of experience.
- You are unsure of what industry you should be in.
- You have never been interviewed and are not sure about preparing.

Career advice for you.

BUSINESS TIPS FOR FRESH COLLEGE GRADUATES

Here are some business tips for recent college graduates that will help you choose a career path that is right for you and land that job out of college that you want.

1. Do Not Let the World Decide Your Path.

Sit down and make a list and a plan of your ideal situation. Ask yourself:

- What type of work do you relish doing?
- If you were not getting paid, what kind of work would you enjoy doing?
- What activities in your past have been responsible for your success?

Making a plan will help put you on the right path to getting a great job.

2. Informational Interviewing

Before an interview, research the company and overall industry you are interviewing for. When you have your consultation, you will be able to tell the interviewer about the industry and ask questions such as: "Where do you foresee this corporation going in the next 3 to 5 years?"

The more questions you ask, the more you control the interview. Do not approach the interview as applying for a job. Consider it as doing an investigation to see if the company or even the industry is right for you. Sometimes you will find that you do not care for either. What you want from a first interview is information.

This information includes:

- Information on what you will be doing.
- Information on the company and company culture.
- Information on the industry and the main industries competitors.

Investigate the Company Fully Before You converse

When you have an interview talk, you must do extensive research on a company. For a one-hour consultation, you should do 3 hours of research into the company.

When you research the company, look at these things:

- Who will be interviewing you?
- The company's website.
- The industry the company is in.
- Does the company have the main competitors? If so, who?
- The products they sell.
- The company's cultures.

Find out as much as you probably can about the group before your interview. You will ask questions about the business, the industry, and the people and get much more out of the initial consultation.

3. Select Your Boss with Care

Make sure that you are convenient with and like your boss. Your boss will influence your pleasure, enjoyment, and success in your career more than anyone else.

4. Request for a little bit More Responsibility

When you finish an assignment at your new job, do not sit on your hands, waiting for someone else to give you a new task. Ask for more responsibility.

What Happens When You Request for More Responsibility?

- Your employer grows to trust that you can do it if there is a job that needs to be done.
- The more duty you ask for, the more you will be rewarded.

Asking for more responsibility will break your career open.

5. Choose Something You Love Over Money

This is a time where you can get to know yourself and find what you love to do. This may be hard to think about in the short run, especially if finding a job is hard.

But think about this, would you instead end up in a career that you hate and earn lots of money or be doing something that you truly love for the rest of your life, earning less money?

6. Visit These Job Sites for Leads on Acquiring A Job in Your Field

There are hundreds of job websites that you can use to look for jobs. I have included a few here:

- LinkedIn
- Indeed
- Simply Hired
- Monster
- Craigslist

7. Your Education Never Ends

Do not worry. This is a good thing. You will always be schooling on new items, reading new books, and developing yourself to be the very best version of yourself. You will be schooled in new facets of a position plus gain expertise plus knowledge. Be open to this change.

8. Use Social Media for Networking

There are many opportunities to network. Social media websites like LinkedIn make it easier than before to get in touch with professionals in your field. Many companies who are hiring scout actively for young professionals individuals on LinkedIn. Certify that you have an updated resume and accomplishment list placed on your profile or your portrait.

Use Facebook to network with your peers from the university. Perhaps they also know a person in an industry you would like to work in.

9. What Microsoft, Hulu, Including Julep Executives Have to Say

"The capability to learn quickly and adapt promptly is critical no matter what role you're going in for."

— JULIE GREEN, VP OF DIGITAL
AT JULEP

A panel of tech executives at Western University's

Leadership forum discussed career advice for recent grads.

10. Stay Positive

Always think positively. Remember these two tips when you go for an interview:

- Your interview starts in the parking lot.
- Your examination ends when you leave the building.

Even if you are upset in the interview process, always keep a positive outlook.

Preparation, experience, and a positive perspective will eventually lead you to the perfect job for you.

I hope you enjoyed reading this book!

If you haven't done so yet, I would be incredibly thankful if you could take 60 seconds to write a brief review on the platform of purchase, even if it's just a few sentences!

Your feedback will be a huge help in helping other readers benefit from the information in the book.

You can also contact us by sending an email to tcecpublishing@outlook.com

Like us on https://www.facebook.com/tcecpublishing/

Join our Facebook page : https://www.facebook.com/groups/800312427190446 to stay updated on our next releases!

See you there!

CONCLUSION

Have you have been in the same position for years as your work colleagues slowly climb the corporate ladder? Do not look for the reason in your environment, but in yourself because most employees stand in their way during career advancement. Take responsibility for yourself, get out there, climb the ladder, and get the career you want. Anything is possible if you use all the tips and advice in this book.

Technical competence is not enough to ensure that your work colleagues do not pass you by. If you want to get ahead, you must show a high level of commitment and continuous development. Always choosing the easiest route is a typical career killer. Taking responsibility for your behaviors and mistakes is not always easy, but it is crucial for your professional future. Sometimes even the little things are enough to have lasting damage to your career. Do not let yourself get stuck in a rut.

A good saying goes, if you love your career, you will never feel like you've worked a day in your life. Do what you love, and do not settle for less!

OTHER BOOKS YOU'LL LOVE!

1. Healthy Habits for Kids: Positive Parenting Tips for Fun Kids Exercises, Healthy Snacks and Improved Kids Nutrition
2. Mini Habits for Happy Kids: Proven Parenting Tips for Positive Discipline and Improving Kids' Behavior
3. Financial Tips to Help Kids: Proven Methods for Teaching Kids Money Management and Financial Responsibility
4. Life Strategies for Teenagers: Positive Parenting Tips and Understanding Teens for Better Communication and a Happy Family
5. 101 Tips for Child Development: Proven Methods for Raising Children and Improving Kids Behavior with Whole Brain Training

REFERENCES

[1]   https://www.psychologytoday.com/us/blog/
unified-theory-happiness/201807/7-ways-cope-
people-who-want-bring-you-down

[2] https://www.psychologytoday.com/us/blog/living-
single/201402/10-steps-getting-over-humiliation

[3]   https://workplaceinsight.net/over-three-quarters-
of-women-and-more-than-half-of-men-experience-
sexism-at-work/

[4]   https://workplaceinsight.net/over-three-quarters-
of-women-and-more-than-half-of-men-experience-
sexism-at-work/

[5]   https://www.equalrights.org/issue/economic-
workplace-equality/discrimination-at-work/

[6]   https://www.equalrights.org/issue/economic-workplace-equality/sexual-harassment/

[7] https://www.lifehack.org/articles/communication/8-benefits-identifying-your-values.html

[8]   https://thriveglobal.com/stories/the-power-of-writing-down-your-goals-and-how-to-do-it/

[9] https://www.thebalancecareers.com/tips-choosing-best-job-2060998

[10]   https://www.thebalancecareers.com/steps-to-choosing-career-525506

[11]   https://www.recruitday.com/blog/fresh-grads-guide-job-hunting

[12] https://guthriejensen.com/blog/tips-to-help-new-graduates-get-employed/

[13] https://www.topresume.com/career-advice/5-tips-to-help-students-prepare-for-their-careers

[14] https://www.topresume.com/career-advice/5-tips-to-help-students-prepare-for-their-careers

[15]   https://www.ceu.edu/article/2019-03-29/how-choose-your-thesis-topic

[16] https://www.careeraddict.com/5-benefits-for-students-who-work-part-time-jobs

[17] https://www.quora.com/What-can-a-high-school-student-do-to-prepare-for-their-future-career

[18] https://www.nap.edu/read/19401/chapter/17#429

[19] https://www.allaboutcareers.com/careers-advice/postgraduate-study/professional-qualifications

[20] https://www.jobstreet.com.ph/career-resources/6-reasons-youre-getting-hired#.X51rZ5DivIU

[21] https://www.livecareer.com/questions/2953/what-s-an-unsolicited-cover-letter#:~:text=An%20unsolicited%20cover%20letter%20is%20a%20letter%20that%20expresses%20interest,not%20have%20a%20job%20opening.&text=Since%20you%20are%20writing%20this,inquiry%20to%20a%20specific%20person

[22] https://hk.jobsdb.com/en-hk/articles/10-basic-but-powerful-resume-writing-tips-for-fresh-graduates/

[23] https://www.indeed.com/career-advice/interviewing/job-interview-tips-how-to-make-a-great-impression

[24]   https://www.weforum.org/agenda/2015/06/21-things-you-should-do-on-your-first-day-of-work/

[25]   https://jannalynnhagan.com/blog/2015/8/4/making-a-successful-transition-from-student-to-employee

[26]   https://www.fnu.edu/smooth-transition-student-employee/

[27]   https://social.hays.com/2020/01/29/transition-student-life-to-working-life/

[28]   http://www.inspiringinterns.com/blog/2016/11/how-to-adjust-from-being-a-student-to-an-employee/

THE MOTIVATED YOUNG ADULT'S GUIDE TO CAREER SUCCESS AND ADULTHOOD

PROVEN TIPS FOR BECOMING A MATURE ADULT, STARTING A REWARDING CAREER, AND FINDING LIFE BALANCE

DEDICATION

This lovely book is dedicated to all the beautiful students all over the world who, over the years, have passed through the T.C.E.C young adult's program. Thanks for the opportunity to serve you and invest in your colorful and bright future.

Your free gift!

Voucher ID: NGH0001

As a way of saying thank you for purchasing this book, I am offering you a free gift at the end of the book

You may very well be a grown-up, but the odds are you are not. Yes, most of us are walking about in grown-up bodies, but that does not make us adults.

As much as we are excited about being adults, it is not usually as easy as it seems, but many do not know that because we are not adequately educated.

Add to the fact that it is complicated to become an adult. The main reason why this is so tricky is that there are few role models. E.g., look at a list of world leaders and show me one person who is a real adult. Perhaps some of the lesser-known leaders would qualify. If you are a grownup, then you have accomplished something incredible.

However, we cannot help but realize the bitter truth about being an adult, and it is not usually easy to accept.

Our parents did not tell us that we would have to be responsible for ourselves and that the little things we used to ignore would require our effort as adults. We were not told all of that.

We were not told that being an adult would require a high patience level, especially in our careers, and attaining other set goals.

I am sure many of us grew up to realize these things on our own, and we were quite taken aback. The glitz and lure of adulthood is not such a fantastic ride.

We could go on and on with it, but then that is not the point. This book is here to provide answers to these questions as well as every other thing that is required to being a responsible and successful adult in life.

The truth is that not everyone would be the ideal adult because everyone is different. However, getting this book is taking a step towards becoming the perfect adult everyone expects you to be.

One thing to be noted is that getting this book is not just the end. After all, it is not a magical book that just transforms you from mere reading. Therefore, reading to understand is very important.

Once you understand and practice what you have read here, you are way ahead of others and on the journey to being a well-adjusted adult capable of handling with ease whatever it is that life throws at you.

I do not want to spend a lot of time convincing you to get this book, but if you do get it, you are on the right path to being that adult you have always envisaged yourself to be.

We are about to embark on a life-changing experience with this book, and I am excited as you are. I wish you good luck.

Let us get started!

After reading this book, please feel free to leave a review based on your findings and how useful the book was to you. I would be incredibly thankful if you could take 60 seconds to write a brief review on the platform of purchase, even if it's just a few sentences!

WHO IS AN ADULT?

*S*uppose I say an adult is a person who is 18 years or older unless the matter is drinking legally, in which case an adult is someone 21 years or older. That is a start. But we are not so much interested in legal definitions as changing conceptions of who an adult is. You could argue that unless we know who an adult is, we do not know who a person is or who a human being is.

Aristotle said that to know what the thing is, one needed to know its final cause. For example, I could display to you a corkscrew, a piece of wood with a spiraling wire descending from it. I would explain that it is for removing corks from wine bottles. That is what it was invented and created for. That, for Aristotle, was its final cause.

The Final Cause of a living organism is the function that the organism performs typically when it reaches maturity. The form or structure it develops and evolves through childhood should help it accomplish these functions well when it reaches maturity. To understand and get what humans are, we need to know what we expect fully grown adult humans to be.

> *A couple had a beautiful bouncing baby girl*
> *called Amy. She was so young and fragile that*
> *she had to depend on her parents for every-*
> *thing, especially her mother. From accommo-*
> *dation to feeding and all other provisions,*
> *Amy solely relied on her parents.*
> *They decided what she wore, the school she*
> *went to, and even the type of friends she made.*
> *It is very safe to say that Amy is still a*
> ***CHILD.***

An adult is a person who takes 100 % responsibility for his or her life and situation. That is, nothing is someone else's fault. The words "It's not fair" do not occur to you. An adult or grownup takes responsibility for his or her emotions. In other words, no one else makes you feel the way you do. An adult is honest with himself or herself. That is, no self-deception, no pretending. You see people and situations as they are and find a way to respond to them.

> *Amy has grown to a particular age, and she does not want to be associated with the term 'child' anymore. After all, she is 18 and is legally an adult. Therefore, she can decide what she wants to do with her life. She has gotten to an age where she can make some significant decisions without her parents' and even friends' influence. However, is this what it takes to be an **ADULT?***

You do not just become a grown-up when you turn eighteen. Adulting is a process. It takes many trial and error and stern reminders or hints from life and expired relationships. Although we sprout, grow up and acquire tools, responsibilities, and trades, deep inside, we are still children who snap back often. Whenever or at any time we encounter resistance or triggers, our child rears its reactive head. We pout, whine, and complain. Adulting is a practice. It takes years and years to become aware of our child and stop pulling from whom we used to be once or how we were handled and treated.

Adulthood is not centered on a particular age but one's ability to work and handle whatever life throws at him or her. Your ability to handle situations, whether emotionally, mentally, and even psychologically, are essential factors that will determine how much of an adult you are. If your reactions to situations are always emotional or irrational, it does not matter if you are 70 years old. You would still be a child mentally.

Not long ago, Mrs. Harrison realized that she had not entirely made the transition to adulthood. She had attained an adequate level of emotional intelligence. She was keenly aware of her emotions and controlled them very well. Where she fell short was her lack of sensitivity to other's feelings. She thought she was sensitive and even prided herself on her ability to "see" others. She thought of herself as a mature adult, after all.

In her work, she often advised people on what to do and how to do it. She often facilitated processes for various groups. She wrote and published three books. She gave lectures on personal responsibility, leadership, and spirituality. Yet, she came to realize that she was not a 58-year-old adult. She was more like a 15-year-old with 43 years of experience. Most 15-year-olds are at the center of their universe. "Everything revolves around them." Although she practiced unselfishness and often cared about others, her perspective was a center of attention.

As a center of attention, she expected people and situations to cater to her. She was often frustrated with other people. When someone told her something personal, she related it to herself rather than truly understanding them. As children, we are all centers of attention. We expect the "adults" in our respective lives to provide for us to give us what we need. She did not expect people to give her food or money, but she did expect people to meet her emotional needs.

And she had it on the authority of her "grown-up" son that she had not been an adult either. He is 35 years old and becoming an adult. He has never met a good role model--not his parents, none of his teachers at secondary/high school or university, no managers in the workplace, and his field, which is Art, no artists that he has met. He had to figure it out on his own.

"Me too," said Mrs. Harrison.

Although her son certainly has catalyzed her.

Perhaps the most significant realization has been that her ego is like that of a child. All egos are children. Anyone who is run by their ego cannot function as an adult. The ego is the center of attention. An adult is a center of influence. That is, as a center of influence, you realize that your thoughts and emotions have a ripple effect. This ripple effect has a lot of influence as well as an impact on people around you.

Everything that you think, feel, say, and do affects the people and the situations around you. This is a change in perspective from *"How is everyone and everything affecting me?"* to *"how are everyone and everything affected by me?"* It is an understanding that life is not happening to me. I am creating it with my every thought, with my deeply embedded assumptions, values, and beliefs. The meaning we perceive in people and things are the meaning we have assigned to them.

An adult questions assumptions--his or her own and everyone else's beliefs too. In other words, as an adult, you think rather than parrot the thoughts of others. It is difficult to subscribe to people's prefer-ences if you are an adult. If you do subscribe, you probably do not subscribe to all of it. Everything that shows up in both your thoughts and in your life gets questioned: "Is it true?" If you are truthful, you will find that most of them are not. You will find that most of everything people hold to be true is being made up apart from the Bible, which contains THE TRUTH.

As you enter adulthood, it will seem to be a struggle at first. You are releasing cherished beliefs. You are letting go of your need for approval, for control over others, and your habit of accepting "truths" that just are not true. For example: "You can have whatever you want!" Many have spoken that "truth," but it is not valid. You cannot have whatever you want. There-fore, so many of us got frustrated after trying so many books and programs without success.

You can have what you TRULY want. You can only if you know what you want, so ask yourself the following questions, *what do you truly want? What is important to you?* Do not answer that question too quickly. These are not questions that you just answer sparingly because you feel you have the answers readily available. Set aside your fiction and your goals. Get quick, and ask the question. What do I want? Listen within. Keep asking if need be, given that we most identify with our egos, an excellent way to inquire may be: "Not my will, but thy will be done."

Once your answers begin to flow, act on them. That is the other trait of an adult; the ability to move forward courageously, to do what you are instructed to do from inside. Perhaps the most important thing that we could say qualifies us as an adult, the ability to listen to our inner man and do something based on internal instincts and not due to some external factor/influence.

So, are you an adult or not? Be honest. If you are, you already know it. This book does not evoke any emotion for you. Reading this book does not automatically make you an adult, nor does it qualify you as a responsible one. You alone know the things you feel as you read this book.

So, deep down, if you know you are not, then maybe it is time to start growing up. It is worth the effort. The reward is freedom and the power of 100 % responsibility. The bonus is the joy you get knowing that you cannot be anyone's victim. You will find out that you need not participate in any more dramas or soap operas in life. And as you release your fears, worries, resentments, and disappointments, that there is a stronger voice within you that will guide you.

Instead of hoping certain things will happen for you (as children do), you trust that your conscience, which is the door to your spirit, will guide you well. You will form intentions from what you have fed your heart with, and those intentions will bubble up from within you. You will sense knowing that the path you intend is the right one. You will accept, but not judge, that most others are still children and do your best to be helpful--to be the role model we so desperately need.

Thus, life is all about understanding what to do, where to do what, and when what you need to do will occur. Adulthood may be a difficult phase, but it is not a license for you to blame and criticize others when things do not go your way.

Being an adult is much more than just dressing smart and earning money from work. Adulthood comes with many responsibilities and sacrifices to be made along the line so before you call yourself an *adult*, ask yourself if you are ready to go through all of these.

If you feel you are, you must ascertain and judge if you are mentally and emotionally prepared because being an adult is not just limited to the things we think we know, so you have to bear all of these in mind.

I am sure that you have a more enlightened grasp and understanding of who an adult is from all you have read in this chapter. Having a vision of this concept in mind will help you navigate the adulthood phase quicker.

WHEN DO YOU KNOW YOU ARE AN ADULT

The age when you become an adult is open to interpretation in many households. There are those 12-year old's who think they are 17 and then 35-year old's who prefer to stay at home, being looked after and avoiding the personal and financial responsibilities of being independent.

In most countries, adulthood can be said to have been attained between the ages of 16 to 18, with 18 being the generally accepted legal age for being an adult.

Astrologically, the late '20s are deemed to be the age when young people enter adulthood. This often equates to when they start settling into making responsible lifestyle choices, committing to a career, home, relationship, and perhaps even starting a family.

This time can be delayed by years spent at university, taking a gap year, the impact of student debt, establishing a career or business, saving the deposit to buy a first home - any of these can defer leaving home and becoming independent.

However, this appears not to be so for many people out there, which poses the question, *so when do you know you are an adult?*

I asked some teens to tell me what they think being an adult is and how they will know adults. Here is what they said:

Angelica C

I will know that I am an adult when I can live on my own when I am fully capable of surviving independently. I will no longer depend on shelter, food, transportation, and money from my parents. I feel that an adult does not mean that you just turn eighteen. For me, being an adult means someone older than eighteen who is capable of living without expenses from one's parents. I think that many people, especially teenagers, think being an adult means turning eighteen because you are "free." However, just like Uncle Ben from Spiderman says, "With great power comes great responsibility." As one gets older, one obtains more responsibility. When a teenager turns eighteen, they have a lot of responsibility: paying for their car, home, school, food, and other necessities. To me, if a teenager can take those responsibilities, then they are considered an adult. I honestly believe that many Hispanic teenagers who are eighteen or older are not adults because most of them, at least in my neighborhood, still depend on their parents. I plan on being an adult when I turn eighteen and graduate high school. Hopefully, I can receive scholarships to pay for my college education and dorm costs. If that works, I will consider myself an adult because my parents will not pay for anything.

Maria V

I will know that I am an adult when I find my passion in life. What I mean by "passion in life" is what you want to do in life. For exam-

*ple, when you are little, you want to be a fire-
man, policeman, doctor, teacher, etc. ... As you
get much older, you start to see what you are
interested in. Once you hit secondary/high
school and have a career that calls for your
attention, then I think you are mature because
you have a future ahead of you, you are
thinking of college, and you know that you are
making the right decision.*

Andrea G

*I have no slightest idea how I will know I am
an adult. I asked my friends around me when
they all thought they would feel like a grown-
up, and they all said, "I don't think you can
ever stop growing," "You may get old, but you
never stop growing spiritually, emotionally,
and mentally." For me, I found that to be very
inspirational. When you think about it...It is
true, there is no point in your life that
someone says you are an adult. I believe that
it is just a way to label people and target a
specific age group.*
*I will consider myself an adult when I feel
old enough, have kids, am married, and have*

a job that I love. I think this way because there is no evidence that you are an adult when you turn a certain age. I think people say that you are an adult when your brain fully matures, and it has reached its peak, but boys and girls grow at different rates, and you cannot assume all girls and all boys. Another thing is that everyone has a distinct personality, biochemistry, and hormones.

There can be times of mixed emotions when we are faced with adulthood. When we are faced with reality, we need to be serious and provide a voice of authority or reason. Our children may have said or done something wrong, naughty or dangerous, and as much as we would love to laugh along with them, we really ought to act as responsible adults and chastise them for their behavior.

Neither do we want to pass on unfortunate habit patterns to our children, like an extreme over-reaction to spiders or cockroaches, or have them witness negative traits and characteristics that we might have imbibed from when we were young too. Being a good role model is essential when we are adults because everything we do is reflected in others' attitudes and behavior.

Or maybe that our parents are becoming increasingly frail and reliant on us, so that we must be the responsible adult who determines what happens to support their care, maybe by taking out a power of attorney or signing a DNR (a do not resuscitate order) in case they become infirmed or when they are gravely ill. Parenting our parents pushes us into serious adult mode.

What about our relationships? Often, they evolve with each person acquiring their regular tasks. One may tend the garden, balance their finances, and look after the car while the other attends more domestic chores. But what happens if one person goes on strike or, for some reason, fails to undertake their agreed duties. Sometimes, when things do not go our way, we may see our inner person emerging by way of sulking, temper tantrums, retaliation, and tears - hardly an adult response!

Now, this is by no means invalidating your emotional response to things. Of course, it's fair to get angry sometimes. You are allowed to cry sometimes when things are not going your way, whatever it is, you are only human to feel that way, but what qualifies you as an adult is how well you manage these emotions, especially how you show these emotions to others.

There are ways that you can use to handle such situations without losing control. You must understand that there are approaches to these things, and you must navigate these feelings. Discussing how we feel about what has happened or gone wrong and then negotiating a way forward can be a better response. Maybe it is a good time to redefine our roles, delegate several tasks, or buy additional help, bringing communications back onto a more adult footing.

And do not forget the childlike joy in life that we may never want to lose, the excitement at visiting a funfair, hearing an ice cream van, seeing the first snowfall of the year, running along a beach. Nurturing our sense of innocence and treasuring it adds another dimension to being an adult. That sense of fun, elation, the joy of being alive is an exceptional part of finding balance in being an adult.

For Jonathan, it was hard settling into adulthood. For him, it was not about starting up a career, family, or even buying a property. It started when he had to go to college at 17.

Coming from a family where things were not so good, it was upon him to cater to some needs without waiting for his parents' input. He had to shuffle between school and work over at some drugstore close to the campus over at college. At 17, he had learned some hard lessons and gone through some experiences that even some adults would never have dreamt of ever experiencing. It did not matter that he was young and all. Life had dealt with him with some hefty blows.

Therefore, you need to understand that your age does not necessarily determine if you are an adult or not, so you must be able to decipher whether you want to identify with the term 'adult' as you attain a certain age.

As much as the thought of being addressed as an adult can be quite thrilling, it can also be slightly frightening for some people. At such times, they are not sure they should be referred to as an adult just yet.

When do you know you are an adult? There are a lot of disagreement on the right time to associate with the term adulthood. From what we have read so far in this book, one thing is for sure: maturity is subjective and has different meanings and explanations to other individuals.

There is no definite time stated for an adult, and they're probably will never be. However, emotional, mental, social, psychological, and financial growth can be the criteria in which one can assume the role of being an adult.

*T*here was a time in our lives where we looked at the adults back then and wished that we were all grown-up. In essence, we all wanted to be ADULTS so badly that we would even go as far as playing dress-up and imitating the adults in our lives.

However, as we start to attain puberty and move through the teenage phase, we begin to realize that things are not as they appear to be, and it begins to feel like the whole idea of adulthood was a sham

As we grow up and assume the much-anticipated role of being an adult, we start to realize that there are some harsh truths that our parents did not talk to us about.

As this reality starts to hit you in the face, you will understand why some adults always seem to be unhappy with themselves and others around them. They are not bitter people; they find it more challenging to cope with adulthood's harsh realities.

It is essential for you as a young adult to understand and know some of these hidden truths about the world of adulthood as knowing these will better equip you with adequately coping with these hidden and often hard truths about adults' world.

First, **you will realize that you start to lose touch with everyone and everything.** Do not get this wrong. You are not sinking into depression or coming down with a mental illness. It is just one of the bitter truths about adulthood.

As I began to step into the threshold of being an adult, I started to feel very differently about some things. At first, I thought I was depressed because I did not understand why I did not react to something with as much enthusiasm as I used to when I was relatively young.

It was or is probably the same for you. Things and people that used to interest you and make you happy do not appeal to you anymore, and you are not easily excited about hangouts, holidays, and even gifts.

You will notice that you do not talk to people as much as you used to. Some friends would fade to the background as everyone would become busy working and living their lives. While it can be a painful experience, it is usually bound to happen.

Trust me. You are not losing yourself. You are going through a phase that no one prepared you for. These are some of the things that you probably never knew would happen as you grew older. You do not have to be friends with people you grew up with.

As a famous African proverb says,

> "Twenty friends cannot be friends for
> twenty years."

Therefore, it is essential to know that these things would happen. People drift apart and lose the connection you once had. However, you must note this and learn how to handle this so that you do not end up pushing people away and severing significant ties with those that matter.

Another hidden truth about adulthood is that **although maturity comes with freedom, you will not always be free**. We are all excited and happy at the prospect of being adults and being open to doing whatever we want without interference. You will, over time, come to realize that it is not what it seems. As much as you have attained freedom as an adult, you will discover that you are not free to do what you want.

"Immediately, I got off of college and started to work. I quickly realized and visualized that things were not going to be as I envisaged them to be. I had always thought that being an adult meant I had more freedom to do whatever I wanted, have fun, and stay out if I wanted. I was soon caught up with work that I barely had time for something as easy as grocery shopping, talk more of even going out, or hanging out with friends.

Whatever free time I had was spent sleeping in bed and trying to prepare myself for the next week of work. It was like I was free to do the things I wanted but still did not hold onto my freedom. Nobody ever told me it was going to be like this "

— DAVID OWEN

You might have the finances to go all out, but there is no time to have fun because, as an adult, the fun would be the last thing on your mind as working and daily living would take away your time mostly.

As a young adult, you will also realize that **you are responsible for yourself and accountable to others**. As you start to live the life of an adult, you will realize that those little things you used to take for granted do take a tremendous effort.

For example, you always used to go to your parents for money to get stuff, and when you did not get your demands met, you would throw tantrums and think they purposely do not want to help you out.
As a grown-up, you will start to see things from their perspective and understand the reasons for their actions. As you start earning,

*you will realize that extravagant spending is
not ideal.*

One other thing is that you will realize that people now look up to you, and you owe them explanations for every rational and irrational decision you make, especially your family members.

Therefore, you must be responsible for your dealings and take actions that will prove you can handle adulthood and increase the confidence others have in you.

Another hidden truth about being an adult is that **you start to say NO more often**. As a child and growing teenager, it was always easy to agree to things people around us want, like choosing to go to the mall because your friends want you to even when you know that you have assignments to work on.

We all had moments like this where we prioritize what our friends wanted because we could not say NO. Well, adulthood changes all of that. You learn to say "no" a lot, especially to close friends and family members.

I remember the first time with my friend. Jenny

and I had been friends from 3rd grade. We were very close and did almost everything together. The thing about Jenny was that she always made the major decisions. She decided on the places we went, the people we chose as friends, and all of that. All through high school and even down to college, it was always like that, mostly as we both attended the same university. There were times when I was not cool with some of the things she suggested, but she had a way of making me do the things she wanted regardless. It got to a certain point where I had to tell myself that I could not always do what she wanted. As expected, she was livid and could not comprehend why I was refusing to hang out with her and do the things we used to do together. I tried to let her know that something had to change because we have both grown and had to live our lives as different individuals now with responsibilities to handle. Things went sour between us, and the friendship was not as strong as it used to be, but I did not regret telling her NO because I knew it was the right thing to do at that point.

Now, this may make you feel self-centered and appear too mean, but that is just one of the things that come with being an adult that you never knew would happen. As an adult, you will understand that learning to say NO sometimes is suitable for your emotional, physical, and mental wellbeing.

Finally, one more truth about adulthood is that **we realize that we become more selfish with our time.** This may look weird because while growing up, we have always been taught that being selfish is bad. While this is true in some sense, you realize that it is necessary to be selfish as an adult.

By selfish, I mean you start to cherish the little time you get to yourself. Rather than jump at every opportunity to go to an outing, event, mall, etc., you start to realize that you would rather chill at home, cuddled up in bed with a blanket and popcorn, and just watch your favorite movie.

Jessy recently opened up about not having a social life at all, especially since she clocked 26. When she was asked why she said she recently started feeling old as little things no longer interest her. She has begun to prefer binge-watching movies to hanging out with

*her friends. She said she had begun to feel too
old lately. She wished she could go back to
being a child.*

It is funny but real, and I am sure that as adults, we all feel these things, and even as young adults, you may have started to experience these feelings in small doses. You cannot always give to others without giving to yourself. Therefore, it is okay to put yourself first before others.

You must understand that these experiences would not be the same for everyone, and the list is neverending, but for the sake of the book, we will discuss just five of them.

However, every adult would have experienced these things at some point. If you have not, do not feel like something is wrong with you. You must understand that these are just processes of adult life.

All of these are some concealed truths about being an adult that we never knew about. While being an adult can be fun, it will not always be fun but what is important is learning to deal with these truths and knowing that it is all part of being an adult.

ADULT LEARNING

*H*ave you ever thought of asking yourself a question about your adulthood? Have you ever wondered why your adulthood is not as pleasant as studying new skills in your childhood? Do you know you can become a child while learning and an adult while knowing and acting?

One thing should be clear to us: Education is a life-long process from birth till death. There is no specific period when education is going to stop. From the day a child is born till their last breath, they need education for a spectacular memory that will be kept for posterity. Every day we learn new things, and there is never a time where we stop acquiring knowledge. This can be in the form of personal experiences, stories you must have learned from others, and so much more. These serve to educate us, so learning is bound to take place as long as one lives.

An individual who refuses to give herself or himself to proper tutoring has surrendered him/herself to mediocrity. There is nothing as hurtful as watching your contemporaries exploit while you remain stagnant with the baseless excuse that you are old. An enlightened mind is a compelling one, and you are equipped with the power to do things that others did not deem possible. After all, knowledge is power.

Have you ever thought of the logic and reasons why education is almost a compulsory part of everyone's lives? From the time you were born, you were taught to speak, feel, and learn new things even as a child. You were enrolled in school to learn more and become educated. Everything served as a lesson because learning is one of the keys to surviving in our world.

Many people achieve most of their feats in their adulthood stage. It is not that they never wanted to accomplish those things at their prime, but circumstances beyond them pushed it further. Their resilient spirit kept pushing them till they could achieve that which they have dreamed of becoming.

This is not an advocate that you need to wait till you are closer to the grave before you start to achieve. It is just to let you know that there is no stipulated time that learning can stop. It is infinite. Before your birth, people were learning; after your delivery, people learn; after your death, people will learn.

You must understand that part of being a productive individual and being a citizen of any country is to learn a way to give to society and not be a burden to society. In this vein, governments are tasked to provide free education to their citizens, and in turn, all citizens have the responsibility to acquire education for their benefit. It should never be a take-take situation. It should be a give-and-take situation where you have something to offer to the government asides from seeking things you can get from them.

It is also applicable in the way you relate to people around you. Always learn new ways to help those around you and not always seek the things you can get from others. For example, in typical African societies, the children are usually trained to go to school to help the family.

Indeed, children go to school to learn how to read, write, and do math, and they continue to amass new knowledge and skills as they grow older. And after graduating from university, and now as adults, they are expected to get a job or try their hands at putting up their own business and become responsible adults and citizens. But learning is not supposed to stop after graduation; it should continue long after finishing academic pursuits in school.

Bryan D

After I got out of university, I thought that was the end of reading books and staying up all night reading. I had thought that I would not have to bother with anything that had to do with racking my brain mentally. That was not the case because even at work, I learn new things every day, and these things require me to research and know more about them. I understand every day, even when I do not feel up to it. One thing I have learned is that education is not restricted to the four walls of a classroom.

Adult learning should be one of our priorities as education should be a lifelong process, never stopping at one body of knowledge but going through different disciplines to make a person well-rounded and knowledgeable. Of course, this is quite impossible in the real world - no one can know everything there is to know. However, you could always have a reason to want to learn more. That is to have self-improvement and become qualified for more responsibilities, especially at work, to aim for a promotion or a salary increase. It is vital to know everything about a particular subject and, at least, a little of everything.

Adult learning is quite different from what we have gone through as children and during our teens. Young people would lack self-direction and autonomy that allow learning to proceed unimpeded. Adults can direct themselves towards their real goal in life, acquire the basics of life experiences, and possess practical knowledge about family relationships and work responsibilities through their previous formal school education. Adults want to learn something that can lead to realizing their goals, and they would be willing to go through any training if they are relevant to what they are after. Because they are practical, they can focus on lessons proven to be useful in their work line.

We can find many adults today who are willing to learn new skills but are hesitant to take the first steps. They think that there are no more opportunities to acquire new knowledge and much less to live by what they would have learned because they have passed their prime. They are afraid that they will not find any open doors that would lead them to a renewed career path. But this is just not true. You can find plenty of help when it comes to adult learning opportunities. You can find many online offers for career advice that is right for you. You can contact them over the phone or through email and ask for career advice.

We have recently heard stories about older people going back to college and getting their degrees. It goes to show how much schooling and education are essential. There is no limit to what you can obtain and the knowledge you can acquire once you put your mind to it. There are several ways you can make out what you want to achieve.

You can go through self-assessment by asking yourself what exactly is it that you want to achieve at this point in your life. Can you afford to learn new skills and knowledge, or can you afford not to? One relevant question that you should not forget to ask is the timing - is this the right time to take adult education classes? On a personal level, are you disciplined enough to go through the lessons?

Many adult learning courses are designed to take advantage of today's technology, which usually means through online classes that you could access anywhere in the world where you could bring a computer. There is an internet connection. You do not have to sit inside a physical classroom if that is what you are afraid of. Some are designed to let you learn through volunteer work in your community or by researching your local library.

With new technologies and social services such as Google Classroom, HubSpot, Udemy, and other online learning platforms, people, especially adults of any age, can sit from the comfort of their homes and acquire an education that is made readily available to them and receive a certification after that.

WHAT QUALIFIES YOU AS AN ADULT?

How many adults do you know? Who exactly is an adult? My severe and light-hearted response when asked about adults? - *"Don't let the big bodies twit you!"* Adults are neither as universal as you might naively guess nor as rare as you might reasonably expect. That does not imply that there are all that many out there, and what do I mean? If you look up the word "mature" in the same dictionary, you will find "fully developed, as a person, a mind, etc." It seems somewhat circular. Does anyone know what is being described? What are we even talking about?

It is also easy to come across a slew of quotes that ennoble children and ridicule adults. Are all these just so-called that grownups are envious of and yearning for the joyful, carefree, playfulness of youth and employing self-deprecatory humor that is cheaply aimed at adults' mundane responsibilities and muted effect?

Just look at what adults do. Adults usually engage in gainful employment regularly; take care of their self-, wife/husband, family, and extended family care. Adults are answerable for their life commitments, including job, bill paying, house chores, upkeep, and being as good as their word. Adults are held liable for what they sign up to do in their public community / private lives, such as writing, writing, doing, and saying.

Grownups are held accountable for their actions and commitments in life, whether that is in a relationship, marriage, or friendship, in a work environment with meeting both the letter and spirit of their job details and description, and in the community being a worthwhile citizen regarding keeping their house and courtyard kept up, being informed of community issues and well-being in addition to political candidates and public issues, and regularly engaging in the voting proceedings. When you watch what grownups do, this does have a ring of maturity in being fully developed as a person. Being an adult in all these forms is rather a high watermark to meet for almost all of us.

So, you might ask, what is so hard in being an adult after all? Well, to state the pronounced, it isn't one bit easy, and hardly will it be getting more comfortable with all the modern times in which the Western world brings in terms of diversions, entertainments, distractions, mobile devices, gaming platforms/games, internet, speed of life, governmental regulation, dealing with bureaucracies and the exponentially increasing stuff of life to somehow fit into the same twenty- four hours a day, one hundred and sixty-eight hours a week, just like anyone else.

Who has the passionate desirous fire in the tummy? Who has space or time? Is it all to race faster away from all the ego-mind's saber-rattling worries, ultimately of after-life, annihilation, nothingness, or running more quickly toward all the ego-minds dream up is selfish gratifications, greedy attachments, and wants of media-manipulation into supposed needs? It is like being captured in a vice, somewhere amid rock and a hard spot, all orchestrated and choreographed courtesy of one imaginary, abstract, ego-mind or self.

It is proposed that self-responsibility or self-account-ability is the quintessential defining attribute to qualify as an adult. The word responsibility means "response-ability," that is, possessing the ability to respond. Self-responsibility means not only deciding, choosing but further participating in an engaged, responsive, most efficient possible fashion or form in taking responsibility or liability for your entire full life. See the attribute of being responsible for one's individuality as having the capacity, the willingness, and enacting in the behavior (sometimes called "prax-is") of a continuing moment to moment.

Self-responsibility can be displayed and seen in taking care of doing and actioning what you said, promised, plighted, and signed up to do, without any if's, but's, blaming others, rationalizations, reasons, or sniveling excuses for not doing what there is to be done if there is some way within the parameters of reality to do it honorably.

This character feature of self-responsibility is synony-mous with self-accountability. In a like fashion, accountability means "account-ability," that is, owning the ability and capacity to account for your own life. To be self-accountable means to be amenable to the obligations and duties you have in your life by the very nature of being alive as a human being in the web of life on planet Earth. Anyone who is self-accountable answers fundamentally to him- or herself in honoring a code of living, ethics, and honesty that goes to the depth of who every one of us is, on the highest, broadest, and most profound of levels, and ultimately on the indwelling and transcendent Divine realm. It is simple and not easy to ever approach comprehensively to inhabit this vision as much as we can.

While this view is the top of the top, what are the critical building blocks that create a solid foundation for enabling and empowering anyone to inhabit self-accountability or self-responsibility? Consider some keys to get in gear and count on God's word to you and yourself as your authority in life:

Presence

That is, the practice of living in the present moment: Only by turning up in this here-and-now bit can self-responsibility and self-accountability come on-line and be legitimate. Also, add the respectful skill of witnessing, that is, in presence standing aside to observe who we think we are (the imaginary or fake sense of self or ego) to reveal, see-through, and dissolve its fake authority and fear-driven influence.

Honesty

That is, sticking the straight-up, nothing left out, truth in life: Purely by playing with a full-deck in being a stand-up guy or person can anyone take responsibility and accountability for his or her own life.

Stalwart

That is, exhibiting reliable, stable, and disciplined words and actions: When anyone has honest traversed an extended learning curve, much like schooling in the trenches of long, challenging, and smart job and often as a pupil with one or more mentors, any abilities truly built and owned communicates a reliable, stable, disciplined and an aware sense of oneself in having some clear idea what makes you tick.

Congruent

That is, words, actions, body language, facial expression, and tone of voice all communicate the same message of clarity: When one's being and the whole body sends an undivided message and a singular across all levels of expression, what gets transmitted is something more significant than the sum of these parts-it communicates trust and confidence that what is seen, heard, and experienced is more real, authentic, and accurate.

Not knowing and being open

To bring the maturity to full value, not knowing and staying wide open and prone to changes, translates into being available to all inputs, creativity, possibilities, brainstorming, innovation, and perspectives in every stratum of life you might find yourself, all of which are core attributes to yielding and developing self-responsibility and self-accountability.

Win-Win/Non-Zero-Sum Game

Being a mature adult entails shedding the me-me-me primitive ego's connection to itself and performing a much bigger game of what works for everyone, merely a win-win or non-zero-sum game. Here one brings a perspective of no scarcity of anything and a surplus of everything for everyone to meet life's demands.

A rock-solid responsibility in operation to grow

Possibly the rarest character feature and trait on the planet is for human beings to bring-a rock-solid commitment in action to grow. To bring the publicly stated intention to grow, a time and place for this to occur, and indirect activities' follow-through to completion. The three components of a commitment are to be accomplished regularly. It points to a committed person with self-responsibility and self-accountability that are palpably self-evident.

There is no stopping of such a being in any set of circumstances in powerfully harnessing and chan-neling their energies, talents, skills, and abilities in transforming and transcending all obstacles and inhabiting their full creative expression. This may well be the most significant character trait and personality attribute you can bring to any transforma-tional process, whether expressed in a therapeutic process, meeting the highly challenged circumstances relationships regularly present or ineffectively facing, and dealing with change in its multitude of disguises. However, it arises in this present moment.

Apart from that, other things qualify you as an adult. One more thing that allows you as an adult is to craft an identity for yourself is making independent decisions for yourself, especially without external influence.

At this point, you must make conscious decisions on the commitments you need to make, the relationships you want to be in, and the career you would like to take, etc. Making these decisions without influence or control from other people qualifies you as an adult.

While it seems cool to talk about all these things that qualify you as an adult, we must admit that one of the most important traits or factors that can prepare you as an adult is **FINANCIAL INDEPENDENCE.**

You may be so excited to be an adult, but you cannot be an adult without having enough resources to take care of your immediate and future needs. Therefore, young adults need to thrive for financial independence, especially as they are just emerging into the world of adulthood, so that things, especially expenses, would be easier to handle.

You cannot be wholly referred to as an adult if you still depend on your family to take care of your expenses. The reason why every adult is involved in one business or career is basically to source for finances. There is no other feeling that is as liberating as knowing that you do not depend on anybody to fend for yourself.

Financial independence may be essential, but one thing that should not be ignored is that one needs to be patient in all of these. **Patience** is a necessary virtue that emerging adults need to learn. While we all want to do the things that qualify us as full and capable adults, one thing should be understood: things will not always go as planned.

You won't start as the best or most responsible adult out there. You will not be automatically rich and be independent financially overnight. It will take months, and even up to ten years, you will make mistakes. Sometimes you would feel the need to give up, but learn to be patient with yourself in all of these.

As mundane as it sounds, patience is perhaps one of the most outstanding qualities one must possess to qualify as an adult. Learn to be patient with yourself as every day is a day to learn and unlearn things. You are not superhuman, and things will not go your way with the snap of a finger, so you must trust the process and be patient. Peer pressure might be a huge factor as you start to think you are not doing enough compared to others' achievements. Therefore, it is essential to be patient with yourself and the growth process. Therefore, learning to be patient with yourself qualifies you as an adult.

Signs that You have Matured in life

People say that with age comes maturity. However, this is not always the case. Sometimes, those who are younger are even more mature than people who are older than them. Maturity is not weighted or measured by age but by one's understanding and experience in life.

Take a closer look at the clues or signs that shows you that you have become more "mature" than you were before.

- **You are valuing your time.** You will realize that your time is your most valuable resource. Hence, you will make sure that every second is being spent wisely. You avoid sleeping in on the weekends and dedicate your precious time to doing productive things that can help you advance in your profession, grow, and mature in life.

- **You make sure that everything is planned out carefully**. As much as possible, you avoid making impulse decisions. Be it buying a new bag, attending events, and even running your errands, you make sure that everything is planned up to the dot.
- **You prioritize your health and wellbeing**. You no longer care or worry about what other people say about you if you and the people you care about know the truth. You value your wellbeing and inner peace more than the opinion of those people around you.
- **You prefer staying in than going out**. Your perfect Friday night would be to stay at home in your pajamas while watching your favorite shows and eating a box of pizza (either by yourself or with a loved one). A Friday night out in loud places no longer interests you. You simply want peace and the simple joys of enjoying having time to yourself. - If you feel like those points mentioned above, do not apply to you and are still not "adult enough"? What should you do?
- **Transform your mindset**. If anyone tells you that you are not adult enough, it may be because of the way you think and react to

certain things. Therefore, you must transform and change your mindset. Train yourself not to respond to everything that is happening around you. Train yourself not to listen to and spread any form of "gossip." Not everything needs your reaction.

- **Always be mindful of your actions**. Be aware of the things you are doing and how it is affecting others. Remember that the world does not revolve around you, and you must be considerate of the people around you.

- **Learn to take responsibility**. If you made a mistake, admit it. Do not justify your actions even though you know that what you did is wrong, and you have hurt other people's feelings. Take responsibility for your actions and whatever damage it has caused. Ask for forgiveness without justifying what you have done, and make up for your mistakes.

- **Surround yourself with the right people**. You become the average of the five people you spend most of your time with, so make sure you are in the right group. Avoid engaging with too loud people who confidently do "illicit" things and display a reckless attitude and behavior. If you want to be more mature, surround yourself with the people who are focused on doing things that will contribute to their growth, those who have ethical principles and values, and those who would not lead you astray.

RESPONSIBILITY

*B*eing an adult means that you have a specific role to be fulfilling. It is usually associated with finding your purpose for living, which is generally expressed in daily activities or jobs. Unless you are self-employed/employed in a position that matches the ideal career you hope to attain, you are likely willing to file away and possibly forget about the dreams you once had - because society expects that an adult is supposed to be responsible. While you may start with a specific plan based upon a vision you believe God has shown to you, your interests, or your academic achievements, you may have settled for something else because of need or out of necessity.

The reasons for settling for a job that is not within your dreams' parameters may include financial obligations, limited job choices, a competitive job market, or any other number of reasons that leave you with a perception that there are limited options. And once you have settled on and accepted a position, you may likely stay in that job for many of those same reasons. But it is possible that you can have an adequate job, one that pays the bills, and still sustain your dreams of the future because that will serve as a motivating source for change.

What Society Expects

Children are naturally imaginative and usually good with pretending until they are taught about life's realities. They can dream and develop ideas that have no limitations. Their ability to act out scenarios and pretend is not defined by anything other than what they are interested in at that moment. And it may be easy to dismiss their fun because they are "just kids." Children are required to attend mandatory education where they are taught to be dependent upon their teacher, and they learn the skills needed to become productive citizens.

As children become young adults, they have an idea of what it means to be responsible, and they may begin to formulate plans for work after graduation from secondary/high school. Once they have graduated, society considers them to be adults, and then they are now expected to be responsible. They may already be working or just starting in their career - and over time, their dreams can be forgotten in the pursuit of a reliable and steady job, which means they are doing what is expected of them.

Tobi A

When I had graduated from college, I did not know what to do with my life, to be honest. I had studied Mechanical Engineering, but I did not feel like I could find any befitting job in my country. It was hard enough finding a mediocre job, but a career as a mechanical engineer was much harder. That, however, wasn't the scariest part of it all. What was scary was how much my parents and extended family members expected the best from me, and it was hard, knowing I could disappoint them and act beneath their expectations.

Developing a Career Path

A career's start requires focused attention as skills are being learned and productive habits are being developed. Suppose the job was as a result of careful planning and the completion of academic goals. In that case, there will likely be a feeling of satisfaction because a specific plan has been worked through - and it may feel like the ideal career, even if the job is imperfect yet. But then there is a different job choice, one that was born out of necessity, and for whatever reason, that job was the best alternative at the time.

At some point, that person may decide to go back to school to improve their career or change careers altogether. I have met many students like this through my work as an educator. These students have become dissatisfied or unfulfilled in their jobs and recognized a need for change.

Amanda Morty

I had studied Fashion Designing at a prestigious fashion school in my state. Everyone had fought against it, especially my parents, because they could not comprehend earning

money as a fashion designer. It sounded
absurd to them, but I knew what I wanted, and
that was to be a great fashion designer. I was
willing to pick that as a career rather than get
into one where I would wake up each day
unhappy with myself. It was simply unbear-
able to even think of living that sort of life.

My advice to young people, especially graduates who are just stepping into the labor market, is to not rush into things. One thing that should be known and understood is that there is a time for everything. You should never feel pressured simply because everyone expects you to have gotten your career at the start. You are entirely free to take your time and properly think about what you want to do and how to go about it.

It would be best to choose the career that makes you happy and not what pays the most in anything you do. Even having excess money does not often guarantee happiness at all. Ensure that you learn to pick your happiness over everything before taking steps into planning a career path. Whatever career path you take, you must do what suits you.

As Time Goes By

For the person who began with a definitive career plan, it is likely they will not consider other options until later in life, and their dream may stem from a need to do something different - whether it is a change of position or interest in finding a job that provides new meaning for them. For the person who has a job and then, over time, creates a career from it, or they have not found a clear path and frequently switch jobs, they will eventually begin to remember the dreams they once had.

However, those dreams may not align with their present job, or they may feel too far out of reach. But dreams do not need to be forgotten - and they can become a new career set point, provided they can be translated into something realistic and attainable. It takes roughly about ten years in any given profession before you become a professional at it.

Realizing Your Dreams

A dream perception is something you hope to achieve or a person you wish to become. It can consist of that nagging feeling that there is something more you want to do, but it has been set aside for some time. It may also be described as a calling or another job you could now have with a different career path. Either way, a dream causes you to feel unsettled at times - that there is something you have not yet completed. The following are some tools you can utilize to realize your dreams.

It might take some time to realize your dreams, but it is possible with the right efforts. As a young adult, especially one who is willing to be responsible, you can achieve all you set your mind to do.

This will be the right plan for young graduates to become what you envisage as the ideal adult. It is essential to understand some of the points discussed and watch how things would be for you when applying them, especially in your career.

Articulate Your Dream

Begin by talking through or writing out what you believe your dreams to be - and then try to write it out with specific details and include as many changes to it as you can remember. This will help you determine what is causing your feeling of wanting to do more and better understand any job dissatisfaction you may be experiencing now or have felt throughout your career.

Go Back to the Basics

See if you can remember what interested you as a child. Can you articulate a specific memory, and are you doing it now? If not, can you pinpoint when or how the interest was lost? The use of a quiet time journal can help you sort through your renewed thoughts over time and develop a clear picture of the interests you have had and the progress you have made along the way. This process will allow you to resolve any lingering feelings from the past and help you begin a forward focus.

Develop a Realistic Plan

If you find out that all through the process of self-reflection and self-analysis that there is something else you may enjoy doing or another path you would like to take, which goes beyond your present job, then it is time to establish a plan. As you formulate a plan, you will need to consider what you should do to prepare for a new job or career and then set both short-term and long-term goals. For example, consider if you will need to take a class, attend some form of training, or begin a degree program. This allows you to view your future from a position of professional development.

Balancing a Dream and a Job

Visions and dreams are the languages of the spirit, just like English is the language you speak; in a dream, you might be shown a picture or image to guide you for your pursuit. Having a dream is not being silly or acting like a child - although a child's imaginative state of mind certainly has merit. A dream is also more than a representation of an unfulfilled life. It is a desire to do more, grow in your career, and have new experiences. A dream is hopeful as it provides visualization of a goal you can develop. You can be a responsible adult, hold a job, be in a career, and still dream. It is an indicator that your job and employment do not have to become stagnant to you, now that you have an ideal image of an improved future for yourself.

You will find it useful to view your dreams as a source of hope and inspiration. Become inspired to develop a new plan for yourself and have fun as you expand your capacity to learn and capability to create new career goals. People who have forgotten about their dreams, or say they have none, also have not developed a clear vision of their future beyond what they are doing now. But that does not have to be you any longer as you become aware of a new future that you are in control of and have created from your dreams and career aspirations.

Here are five ways you can be a more responsible person:

1. If you have lost your job, do not break down. There are plenty of opportunities on this fertile earth. Surf the web and look where you fit in at the work front and start applying for jobs. Indeed, an excellent job will land on your lap. Give it a little time and be patient.

2. Look after your family through thick and thin. As the saying goes, united we stand; divided we fall. So, stick with your family, share family chores, and share your problems with them. Undoubtedly, several solutions for your issues will lurk up.

3. If you have issues and problems with a co-worker, brainstorm how you can ease their relationship. As it goes, make peace with all men as much as it lies within your power by firstly making peace with yourself; then you

can be at peace with others. Remove resistance. Go with the flow. Start taking it easy at work with all the people involved. Undoubtedly, your problems will start to dissolve only because you cared to take some responsibility for the case.

4. Your prime purpose on this earth is to have a fulfilled life and live the life God wants you to live. We live on earth for a period on probation to acquire life values for the real dwelling invisible to the naked eye for now. Make wise choices, and do not be hasty about them.

5. Do you have children who have become teenagers, and they have become rowdy? They do not listen to you and are incredibly bad-mannered. How do you handle such a situation? Mention it to God in prayer, listen to his counsel, and act on instructions you receive. Take a family vacation. Talk with your spouse about the problem. Discuss it in a family meeting. Discuss it lightly during holidays with your entire family. Reason with them and let them know you are disappointed in their current attitudes and what you expect from them. Remember,

persuasion is better than force. Make the
problem lightly known to them and let them
immerse in it and find themselves. Indeed,
you will start to see them behave and talk in
ways you would like them to do over a short
period.

Financial Responsibility Tips

In this age of irresponsibility, in this time of finger-
pointing, in this era of blaming everyone else for our
ignorance - it is time to step up and be an adult who
has an eye on the future yet enjoys the present
without jeopardizing the foundations we all need and
require.

It is time to be financially and emotionally
responsible.

As much as it may be convenient to act surprised
when people go into debt, it is nothing more than
blind ignorance and massive irresponsibility that
causes a lot of people to spend more than they earn
and to want more than they need, whichever way we
look at it, no matter what occurs to us, we should
always look at the worst-case scenario before
proceeding with any financial decision - whether that

be the decision to have a child, buy a car, or take a vacation.

Mrs. James does not support lending people money, for her, the best she hoped for was to get her money back, and the probability was that she would lose her money and the friendship in almost all cases.

Think before spending, before buying too much that you do not need and do not use. Think. You owe nobody but yourself a financial responsibility.

If we look at all the possibilities and are prepared to take that risk, well then, it will be as it is, and the surprise is taken out of the equation, but the responsibility is not.

Here are some ways you can save money and be financially fit:

1. Develop a financial plan. Identify your long-term goals, save regularly and establish a budget. Make a list of the things you would want to achieve financially and review them from time to time.

Jonah had told himself that he wanted to be a millionaire before the age of 30. He started to

*make plans on how he would achieve this, and
every step and decision he took financially
was usually in line with this vision. Before he
clocked 30, he already had a certain amount
in his bank account that qualified him as a
multi-millionaire.*

2. Save. You are a hard-working young adult, so do not forget to pay yourself first. Set up a savings plan with your credit union or bank. If you can automatically get the savings deposited into your bank or credit union account without doing it yourself, it is easier to build your savings.

This is something I usually advise a lot of young adults, especially young graduates, to imbibe. Learning to save cannot be overemphasized. Set up a savings plan for yourself.

*I had a friend called Josh. We graduated from
college, and as young graduates, we were
excited about finally starting our careers. We
both got jobs and started working right away.
While I always found a way to use up all the
money once I received my paycheck, I never
knew Josh was saving up.*

Barely three years after we started working, Josh invited me over to his house-warming party. He had just gotten an excellent property in a great neighborhood. I was happy yet envious at the same time because I felt somewhat cheated.

I spoke to Josh to let me in on his secret to such quick wealth, and he uttered one word to me, "Save," and I was taken aback by that. I felt like he was not telling me everything, and I urged him to tell me more, but he laughed and repeated the same word.

It turns out that Josh started saving 10 dollars every day. It was hard, but it was something he was willing to do. I had no idea that saving could go a long way in ensuring some sort of financial freedom. It had always been something I took with laxity.

3. Build an emergency safety net. Many financial advisors advise saving up to six months of living expenses in case of an emergency. If you cannot save six months of living expenses, start with one month's payments and regularly increase it. You can begin by stowing away one month's salary for an emergency period.

4. Got an Increase? **Raise** your savings! If you get a surge at work, immediately increase the percentage of your salary that goes into savings. You will not miss the extra money, and you will be growing your nest egg.

> *As I said, you can always save some more. There is no limit to how much you can save. If you were saving 500 dollars monthly, you could increase it to 700 dollars when you get a raise. All you must do is choose a savings plan that would be suitable for you financially.*

5. Manage and build your credit. When you take out a motor car loan or use your credit card, you are establishing credit. The appropriate way to build good credit is to pay your bills on time to prove you are responsible for managing your debt.

6. Pay bills on time. You can avoid late fees and high-interest payments, which can add up and make it harder to pay down the remaining balance. Settling accounts on time is noted and recognized by leading companies and institutions.

7. Read the fine print. Be sure to read, interpret and ask about interest rates and any additional fees when you apply for credit cards, loans, or lease an apartment.

8. Choose the right insurance plan. Whether it is for your health, car, apartment, or life, make sure you have the right coverage and indemnity to cover yourself and your funds.

9. Monitor your credit report. Credit scores are investigated when you apply for a job, buy a car, rent an apartment, etc. That is why it is good to monitor your credit report for any discrepancies or identity theft.

10. Being financially responsible is not just something that you do because others expect you to. You must be financially responsible as that is liberating.

Monitor your spending and watch the way cash flows in and out of your account. You can cut down on unnecessary expenditure and draft out a plan that lets you monitor and know the things your money goes into.

For example, you can draft out a bill like this for your monthly expenses based on your 7000-dollar salary a month.

Expenses for the month: Savings - $ 1000

Food - $1500
Other expenses and maintenance- $ 1700

This is just a rough draft of what you can do with your cash. Depending on how much you receive, you must plan what you spend your money on.

Being emotionally responsible is a dying art that few of us practice, and none of us are taught. Instead, we are lied to, 'miseducated,' and encouraged into the wrong frame of mind from the moment we are born.

We are pushed into a state of dependence instead of a life of independence; because of our childhood brain-washing, the stories we are fed, the movies we devour, and the insecurities we allow to permeate our lives, our relationships end up as emotional wrecks, and our search for love seems to consume us to the point of destruction; instead of us being responsible adults who work on the basis that we need a good foundation (filling your thoughts with the sayings of

Jesus) to build a substantial edifice and that foundation has to be made on an individual who understands themselves and is honest and forthright about their strengths and weaknesses; being reliant upon another human for emotional stability is an anomaly that makes no sense and does not work. We can only be liable for our own emotions.

CAREER

What is your profession? Forget about how you describe this to others for now and just think for a bit about how you define your career to yourself. What does it imply to you to have a career? Is it just your job? Is it something you do to make a living? Is it what you do for funds? Is it your work?

Most people would define a career as more than a job. Above and beyond a job, a career is a long-term work pattern, usually across multiple positions. A career implies professional development to build skills over a period, where one moves from novice to expert within a particular field. And finally, I would argue that a profession must be consciously chosen; even if others exert influence over you, you should still ultimately choose to become a lawyer, doctor, or accountant. If you did not make a conscious choice at some point, I would then say you have a job but not a career.

One of the difficulties I see many people experiencing lately is that they spend much of their days working at a job that is not part of a consciously chosen profession. Once you graduate from university or college and enter the workforce, you do not suddenly learn what kind of career to build. Most likely, you focus on getting a job as your first step after school. And you probably must make this choice in your early 20s. After a decade or two, you have established a work pattern and gathered up some expertise know-how. But at what point did you pause to ask, what is my profession going to be?

Many young adults, especially graduates, are usually quick to jump at any job they are offered without first thinking about the future, especially regarding the career path they want to take.

Sometimes when you question people what their profession is (instead of asking what their job is), the question makes them uncomfortable. Why? This is because they think of a career as intentionally chosen, purposeful, and meaningful, and they do not see those qualities in their trade. Another possibility is that they might feel deep down that their real profession or career lies elsewhere, often the case with most people. The jobs they are in are not the actual career path they should be on.

A countless number of us have been in that situation before, so we can relate to these things to some extent. *I remember one job I had taken simply because I felt the pay was good and I could be happy there. Fast forward six months, and I was already thinking of resigning because it was just not working. Deep down, I knew that was not the career I wanted. I just was not cut out for it.*

Just because you have been working in a field for many months or years does not mean you have to change that work pattern into your profession. The past is the past. You can continue to run the same way and follow that same path into the future, but at any time, you are also free to make a total break with the past and turn yourself onto an entirely new trade path in the future. Ask yourself if you were beginning over from scratch today, fresh out of school, would you still choose the same line of work? If the answer you give is no, you only have a job right now, not a career. Your career lies elsewhere.

Therefore, I would always emphasize that young graduates take their time before choosing the type of career they want to establish themselves. Like I would always say, there is absolutely no reason to rush because your success journey is different from those of others. Make decisions at your own pace and not because other people are already making major career moves. You should have a definite answer to specific questions before choosing the type of career you want to go into.

Think about this for a moment. What is the core of your profession? What is the bigger picture of what you do? What do you contribute? If you work for a big company, then how do your actions contribute to some larger purpose? Be honest with yourself. And do not ignore your company's role in your career; your career depends heavily on contributing to people on your down line. If you genuinely assign a noble purpose to what you do, that is great. For example, if you are working at a grocery store, you might be inspired by the fact that you help feed people. But do not force it if you do not believe it. If you feel your contribution is weak, uncertain, or even hostile, then admit that to yourself, even if you don't immediately plan to do anything about it.

Go behind the labels. Do not stop at defining your career as a computer programmer, lawyer, or doctor. What are you contributing to as a computer programmer? How does your job make a difference in other person's lives? Is it nothing more than a means for you to amass wealth and make money? As a lawyer, do you resolve disputes and spread peace, or do you milk conflict for cash? As a doctor or nurse, do you heal people, or are you just a lawful pusher? What is the essence or core of your line of work right now?

Now when you have your justification and answer, you next must ask yourself, is this you? Is this truly a field that reflects the best of who you are as a person, your talents, and your natural gifts, and you do it with little or no effort?

For example, suppose you see the real purpose behind your current work line as making a handful of children/youth wealthier in knowledge. In that case, nothing is nobler than that, then is that an exact reflection of your best input? Is that you?

If you already have a profession that accurately reflects the best of who you are, that is wonderful.

But if you do not, then realize that you are free to change it. Suppose your career as a regional distributor for a major soft drink manufacturer boils down to pushing sugar water to make people fatter. In that case, you don't have to preserve it in that form.

I assume that if you realize that your current work does not fit who you are, you must choose. You must decide if you deserve to have a career that truly suits you. If you do not feel you deserve it, you will settle for defining your career in such narrow terms as job, money, boss, coworkers paycheck, promotion, etc. No one is imposing on you to take that as your definition of a profession.

As a young graduate trying to find your career path in life, you must understand that it is most likely a life-long decision, so think, ***do I want to be doing this for the next thirty years of my life? Would I be happy doing this in the next 30 years?*** Contrarily, you can choose to grasp or embrace another definition of a career that uses terms like purpose, assignment, calling, contribution, meaning, abundance, happiness, fulfillment, etc. This requires a top-down approach. You first pray to find out what you are created to be, do, and fulfill. Studying the scriptures helps find out your mission to the earth, what your purpose here is, what kind of contribution do you want to make with your life? Once you figure that out through seeking God in prayers, then you work down to the level of how to show and manifest that in terms of the work and tasks you do.

And for many people, the seeming impossibility of that manifesting part is paralyzing. This is especially true for men, who usually take their responsibility as breadwinners very seriously. You see yourself logically having two choices: You could stay in your current job, which pays the bills and earns you a good living, or you could jump into something that fits you better, but you just cannot see how to make it. You have a mortgage to pay and a family who depends on you; you cannot do that to them are all thoughts that come.

The complication is thinking that these are the only alternatives, assuming that you must choose between money and peace of mind or happiness. That theory or assumption is what causes the paralysis against the action. You can also foresee or envision the third alternative of having money and happiness together. That is the most likely outcome. If you do not currently have a deeply fulfilling career to yourself in the sense that you know you are contributing in a way that matters, then deep down, you will sabotage yourself from going too far with it.

You will always know that you are going on the wrong path, and this is going to pump a demotivating slump over everything you try to do in that line of work. You will do your job, but you will never feel that you live up to your potential. You will always have problems with procrastination and weak motivation, and they will never be resolved or solved no matter how many time management techniques you attempt. Your task or job will never feel like a truly satisfying career -- it just cannot grow into that because you have planted your career tree in lousy soil. You will always be cemented and stuck with a bonsai.

But when you get your line of work aligned from top to bottom, such that what you are ultimately contributing is an expression of the best of yourself, the resources will come too. You will be enjoying what you do so much, and you will find your work so fulfilling that turning it into an income stream will not be that hard. You will find a way to do it. Making resources is not at odds with your greater purpose; they can lie on the same path. The more resources you make, the greater your ability to contribute.

But most importantly, you will feel you deserve all the resources you earn. When your specialty or craft is aligned with the best of who you are, you will not secretly think that your continued career success means going farther down the wrong path. You will not hold back anymore. You will want to take your career as far as possible because it interprets who you are. And this will make you far more open-minded and more receptive to all the opportunities that are all around you, financial or otherwise.

But how do you make this transition? Is a leap of faith required? I think of it as more of a leap of courage, and it is a logical kind of courage, not an emotional one. It comes down to deciding how important your happiness and fulfillment are to you. How essential is it for you to have meaningful, fulfilling work that satisfies your mission on earth? Is it OK for you to continue and remain working in a field that does not allow you to add and contribute the very best of who you are? If you spot yourself in such a situation, then your answer is yes -- you have made it OK for you to endure and tolerate this position or condition.

But you see, self-actualizing persons who success-fully make this leap will, at some point, conclude that it is not OK. It is intolerable. They rise and respond,

"Wait a minute here. This is unacceptable for me to be spending the bulk of my time at a job that is not a deeply fulfilling career. I cannot keep doing this. This ends now."

These people "wake up" by realizing that what is most vital about a work line is the high-level view or perception that includes happiness, fulfillment, and living on purpose. Things like money, success, and achievement are a very distant second. But when you work from within the first category, the second category takes care of itself.

Before you have had this awakening, you most likely did not see how that last sentence is possible. And that is because you do not understand that it is nothing more than a choice. You have probably picked to put money above fulfillment in your current line of work. That choice means that you will not have satisfaction. But it is not that you cannot have dignity -- you can select to change your preferences and act on them at any time. The natural selection you made was not to be fulfilled in your current line of work. You bought into the misconception that money is at odds with fulfillment and that money is the more important of the two, so that is all you see. No matter what job you take, you will find that this inference turns out to be genuine for you.

But once you get-up-and-go through the **"waking up"** experience and firmly decide to put fulfillment first, you suddenly realize that being fulfilled *AND* having plenty of resources is also a choice available to you. There are countless ideas for you to do both; you simply must permit yourself to see them. You will realize that you were the one who chose *EITHER-OR* instead of *AND,* while all the time, you were free to select *AND* pick whenever you wanted.

You set the code for your career choices. Most likely, your current average ranks fulfillment and meaningful contribution meager compared to working on exciting tasks and making sufficient resources. But those standards are yours to set. At any point, you are free to say, **"Having a significant and fulfilling career is an absolute MUST for me. Working for money alone is not an option."** And once you make this conscious selection, you WILL begin seeing the opportunities that fit this new standard. But you will never even recognize those opportunities if it remains OK for you to spend all your work time being unfulfilled.

This may not just be in terms of working for a higher authority. Even if you see yourself starting a career as an entrepreneur, you have to also focus on why you are going into that business line and what you stand to achieve in the long run. If you are reasoning or thinking of starting up a company simply because you want to make money, it is safe to say that you are on the wrong path. While making profits is the primary goal of every business entity, you also must think of the impact your business should have on the industry in which you are operating.

I want to drive home this point. Having a fulfilling work line that earns you plenty of resources does not require a leap of courage. It only requires a choice. You just must wake up one day and tell yourself that you deserve both and that you will not settle for anything less. It is not about finding the right job. A career is not something you see; it does not require someone to give you something. You are not at the mercy of circumstances.

A line of work is something you create, something you build and constitute. It means that the job or task you do each day is aligned with what you know to be your purpose; once you start doing this kind of work, even if for no pay initially, your self-esteem will grow to the point where you will become so resourceful and open to new opportunities that you will have no trouble making plenty of money.

By then, the money will not be that vital. It will just be some funds for you to do more of what you love.

WHEN SHOULD YOU BEGIN YOUR CAREER?

Maybe you think you should work between secondary/high school and university to explore and research the world of work. Maybe you should know and recognize what you want to study before going to university so that you have your career path established before you spend thousands of dollars/pounds on your education. Or maybe you should use your university years as the time to explore crafts and specialty options. Each person is uniquely different, and development does not have a smooth or straight path. Career development is no exception. What if I said your career development begins as soon as you learn to walk, talk, and imitate those around you? Would you think I am not making sense, or do you think this makes sense to you?

Specialty advancement is part of human development and improvement. It begins at childbirth and continues as you master or guru more and more skills throughout your life. Today is a different day. Years ago, an individual would decide on a line of work and stay working for twenty to forty years in the same profession for their entire working life. Today, it is not unusual for individuals to change their specialty two or even three times in their working years. Line of work advancement and development does not move forward in a straight line. You need time to understand who you are, what you enjoy, what interests you, what you feel are your strengths and weaknesses, and what kind of lifestyle you want to live. All these things take time to explore, evaluate, and plan. This takes years! When do you begin? You began at birth!

Mrs. Bright, my friend, used to joke that her daughter was forty since she was four years old. As a young child, she showed traits and characteristics that could be considered and expressed career skills. She liked to be in charge, so you perceive that she would be a leader and a take-charge kind of person since she was four. She also loved to help others. She was the eldest of her three children and loved to help her younger sister and brother with whatever they were doing. She was a born leader, a teacher, a helper, a service-oriented type of personality. She knew very early that whatever career path she chose would include working with people, offering some help to others, being in charge, and believing she would be in some type of teaching capacity. As her daughter went through school, she was an excellent and hardworking student. In Middle School, it became clear that she was very good at Science, and she had a remark-able work ethic. When she got to secondary/high school, it was very evident that she was a great science student. During her daughter's sixteenth year, one of her best friends got a type of meningitis that caused her to be unable to speak or move. She was trapped in her own body. Mrs. Bright's daughter watched her friend relearn to use her body. She was deeply and passionately affected by this trauma for her friend. She became interested in the professionals that helped bring her friend back to being a fully functioning person after months and months of rehabilitation. Today, her daughter is an occupational therapist. She could enter university, knowing precisely what she wanted to study, and chose a line of work path that she had been developing since she was a young child.

So, when should you begin to think about a career path? Whether you know it or not, you have been thinking about and developing a career path since you were a small child playing house, playing roles, playing sports, playing an instrument, drawing, singing, building models, listening to music, solving puzzles, playing word games, playing maths games, trying to figure out how things work.

Contrary to what people think, starting your career does not start from a certain 'mature' age. You subconsciously start to prepare for it as soon as you have identified what it is you want to be or do.

Unlike Mrs. Bright's daughter, who knew what she wanted to do from a very tender age, some people usually have no idea what they want till they are well over 30! For these people, they must think and ponder for a long time on what they want to become before finally making a final choice/decision.

Herbert was 32 years and a graduate of Communication Studies from college and had already spent seven years working in an advertising industry before realizing he was on the wrong career path. He enjoyed his work line, but he knew that he couldn't keep at it for a long time. Herbert wanted to be a media personality, which was what he had always wanted to be. Was it too late for him to give off his career? It was not because he soon quit his job and finally started as a small-time radio presenter.

All these activities and actions involve skills you have developed along the journey of your life. Pay attention and consideration to how you spend your time. What do you do in your spare time? What actions or behavior do you take each day that you enjoy? Do you enjoy working with individuals? Do you enjoy working and engaging with data and information? Do you enjoy fixing things, building stuff, making kinds of stuff work? What activity truly interests you?

When you have a couple of hours or days to yourself, what do you do with that time? What brings you fulfillment and enjoyment? Satisfaction? Contentment? What challenges you in a way that stimulates you rather than frustrates you? What activities bring a smile to your face?

When you can answer these questions, ask yourself what careers can offer me these enjoyable opportunities. You will have to work for many years of your life. If you work to earn a salary, your days will be long, tough, and challenging. It would help if you were capable of engaging in work for satisfaction in what you do. You need to be able to feel and sense content in your workplace. You want to enjoy and relish what you do. You want to feel optimistic about what you do, enjoy what you do, and appreciate the wages or that it provides you. You also want to afford the lifestyle that equates.

So, think back over your life or essence and focus on the activities that brought you satisfaction, contentment, and joy. You could be seventeen, twenty-seven, or sixty-seven. Your life experiences have been valuable learning or schooling experiences. Think back to scrutinize and explore your history. If you enjoy working and engaging with people, find a social career. Maybe you want to help others. Explore and research the many medical occupations and see if any of them fit. Perhaps you would love to teach young people and help them develop their minds and skills through education. Maybe you would enjoy and relish business fields where you help people build and run successful businesses.

Maybe you love working with your hands. Perhaps you have always been fascinated by cars and would love to learn how to fix an engine. Perhaps you have always been interested in electricity and would relish being an electrician. If you love working with your hands, then find a career that allows you to satisfy this need in you, releasing the life and light in you to your environment.

Maybe you have always loved being creative. You have loved to tell stories or draw pictures or build things. Perhaps you would love to write, design, or construct buildings. If you are creative, utilize your creativity. Write, draw, design, dance, create, and play music, build, and create. Nurture, nourish, and develop your talents. Nurture your strengths. Be who you are in your character, heart and turn it into your career.

ADULT ATTITUDE ADJUSTMENT

As adults, there are times where everything seems to go wrong, and it just feels like the world is against us. Got a bad hair day, your boss yelled at you because you made a mistake in the PowerPoint presentation, your car broke down when you were already late for an appointment, etc.

All these things make you want to yell, and you find yourself complaining about the thousand ways your life is falling apart, which further sinks you into depression. Anyone who steps in your path becomes a victim of your boiling tantrums.

Suddenly, you find yourself yelling at everyone, you become apathetic, and you start to appear cold to even the people that matter, but at the end of the day, just one question is on your mind, and that is, *"why is all of this happening to me?"*

We all should understand as adults that our attitudes affect our behavior and the way we view things, which, in turn, influences how we communicate with the people around us. The bitter truth is that we sometimes like to blame the circumstances affecting us as the reason why we act in a certain way. It is not always right.

The thing is that sometimes we just have a bad attitude. This is a hard pill to swallow, right? Unfortunately, this is the truth that we most times like to avoid. This is because when you have a bad attitude, you attract negative things to yourself. A negative attitude attracts and produces adverse outcomes, so that difficult time you are passing through might result from your mindset if you take time to look at things constructively.

Of course, there would be signs that would arise that will make you realize that you require an attitude adjustment, and what are some of these signs?

You frequently have the same issues with others.

At times like this, you find yourself being triggered by a particular thing that people do. It sets you off, and you start up a quarrel with them, but the problem might not be them but you. When you continuously have issues with other people because of a particular subject, then it is a sign that you might need an attitude adjustment.

You are never wrong

You never consider the fact that you might be wrong. To you, others are wrong, and you are always right. You think that others need an attitude adjustment and not you.

At this point, you always believe others do not know what they are doing and that only you have the right answer to everything. This is another sign that you must self-adjust your attitude.

I once knew someone like this. He was an acquaintance, and I had to hang out with him sometimes because he was a friend. I noticed from most of the discussions we had because he always felt he was right and made everyone's opinion feel wrong.

It was often discovered that he was wrong, but he never accepted even when the facts were right there in his face.

You always complain about things

When you find yourself always nagging and continually complaining about the things happening in your life, you find yourself being bitter, and this can be dreadful and tiring for the people around you, and that is bad.

People would start to avoid you because they are tired of listening to you throw tantrums about how bad your life is going. You begin to lose friends at times like this because you now appear to be a bitter person.

If you are guilty of this, you must admit that you need an adult attitude adjustment.

All of these and others are just some of the signs that show just how much the problem is with you and not others, and the quicker you are to accept that you need an attitudinal adjustment even as an adult, the more manageable for you.

Now that you might have accepted that your attitude might be the problem, *what are you willing to do about it?* That is where the term ***Adult Attitude Adjustment (AAA)*** comes in.

As an adult in need of an attitude adjustment, there are certain things you need to practice if you want to become a better person and attract positive things to yourself.

First, you must understand that while there might not be a lot that humans can control, we do have control over our attitudes and behaviors. It would be best if you believed that only you have the power to change the things going on in your life, and one of them is needing to accept an attitudinal change. You can control your emotions and how you react to things.

Another thing you must do is to have a **positive mindset.** Nothing surpasses the power of positive thinking. Positive thinking has the potential to turn things around for you once you have mastered the ability to think a good thought.

> *My grandfather was a happy person, and it usually baffled everyone in my family. Even when things were tough and every other person felt sad, Grandpa would walk around humming a tone with a cheerful smile on his*

face. Sometimes it used to piss my mum off because she thought he was merely inconsiderate and not empathetic, but that was not true.

I discussed with him just some years before he died, and I asked why he was always happy. He had said that the reason for his sunny attitude was because he had told himself that he was still going to be positive no matter what happened. Even when bad things happen, he would brush it off and go on with his life. In his words, **'life's too short to be caught, not smiling.'**

That was, by far, the most important lesson I had ever learned in my life.

Your thoughts affect your perception of things and how you would respond to things. When you think about good things, you will find yourself in a good disposition, which generally affects your mood for the day and sets you in a perspective that attracts positive outcomes. It would be best if you understood that once you master the art of positive thinking and possessing a positive mindset, not only does it do wonders for you, it attracts other people to you.

Once you have mastered the power of having a positive mindset, **kindness** comes to you naturally. We cannot begin to overemphasize the importance of being kind to people. Being kind to yourself and others is just another step towards a wholesome attitude adjustment.

Another way to adopt the right attitude is to **identify the emotions** that make you act the way you do. Make sure you understand the feelings that get you easily frustrated and learn to control them. It is crucial for you as an adult to have total control over your emotions because these emotions also greatly influence our thoughts, behavior, and attitudes we portray. Therefore, it is necessary to have a firm hold on your feelings and how you react to them.

Another thing to do is to learn to **admit your mistakes.** This shows a deep sense of humility that cannot be rivaled. Once you are willing to admit your mistakes, it becomes easier to say the word 'sorry,' and you must understand that you cannot always be right.

You must understand that many bad things can happen. You must learn to **accept that things will not always be right.** Adulthood comes with its ups and downs, and while good things would happen, be prepared for the worse and accept that many bad things would occur.

The fact is, there are a lot of adults who are in dire need of an attitude adjustment, but they do not know this, so they walk around with a bad attitude, which makes them appear toxic to others. For these adults, there are a lot of things that need to be learned.

You need to identify these traits that need attention and then work on becoming a well-adjusted adult.

THINGS YOU SHOULD KNOW ABOUT YOURSELF

---

*I*t is essential to have a career plan. This will help you oversee the direction of your career. It will also inform you of the craft skills and knowledge you will need and plan how you may acquire them. One vital element in the development of a career plan is self-assessment. Self-evaluation is crucial because it leads to self-understanding.

Anything you choose to do takes about seven to ten years to start flourishing and be fruitful, so stay at it.

Knowing yourself from your maker's point-understanding is often missing in our day and age. Notwithstanding, this was no less true at the times of the older generation than it is today. How, then, does one arrive at such knowledge? You wonder. This book aims precisely to answer this very question.

Again, the process of arriving at an understanding is a self-assessment. A self-assessment is an honest conversation with your inner being about yourself on what God created you for and to be. It will often assist you in including it in that conversation with other people who know and care about you. Such a process will lead to discovering things about yourself that you might not have been aware of. If you wish to make sure that you plan your work line appropriately, you need to know the kind of person you are.

A line of work strategy needs not to be too compli-cated. How sophisticated, refined and detailed you want to be is entirely up to you. Nonetheless, a sound self-assessment will consider, among others, the following aspects of your life: your values, your passion, your life path, your goals in life, and your current knowledge. Let us now look at each one of these briefly.

Your Values.

Everyone has some things they consider more impor-tant than anything else in life. These are things they would likely always stand for, no matter the circumstances. These things could be some social aspects of life (like family), some political convictions (like women's right to vote), some scriptural doctrines, etc. Generally, values are things for which someone would even consider dying. *For example, Nelson Mandela believed that apartheid was unjust and, in his own words, admitted that he was prepared to perish to see that political system collapse.* Whether they are mindful of them or not, everyone has values and ideals. You should know yours and take them into scrutiny when you plan your line of work and professional direction.

Your Passion/Zeal.

We all have things that we are zealous or passionate about. These are the things we enjoy. They are things we catch ourselves acting on all the time. In a way, we are never bored or tired of doing something we are passionate about. For example, some people enjoy reading. They read all the time, and they do it effortlessly. Others enjoy public speaking. They find great joy and an immense sense of accomplishment when they are vocalizing to a live gathering. Wherever they are, they instantly become the life of the conference. People's passions also keep them awake at night. If you pay attention to your inward being, you will discover what your desires are. They are things which easily excite you. When you are passionate or desirous about something, you always find a way to chat about it, and you can do that for a full day. Your passions should be factored into your work line plan.

Your Life Path

If you do not know and see where you are going, you can end up anywhere!

Create a compelling vision and practice daily to see beyond your struggles. Use positive thinking to help you stay on track and take action so you can see your dream come to life. Day by day, you create your future, make it one that you love, one where you can look back and be proud of your story.

Your Goals in Life

> *"If you do not perceive where you are going, any lane will get you there."*
>
> — LEWIS CARROLL

If you do not have any goals in life, other people will

create them for you. It is not enough to just set goals. You must take the necessary steps to make them a reality.

What do you want to achieve? What are the steps to getting there?

Your Current Knowledge

We all have some knowledge of specific areas. We may have to get such knowledge from previous studies or personal experiences. Sometimes we forget that we have such ability because we take it for granted. However, it is always good for you to think of all the assets (cognitive and others) you already have at your disposal. It does not particularly matter how you got them.

An essential thing is a fact that you do. As a unique bank puts it in a commercial, you may be wealthier than you think. Because of a lack of consciousness of what we already have, sometimes we spend a lot of time, cash, and energy building new foundations when we should build on foundations we already have in place.

I recently took a ride with a friend of mine to a conference. As we were talking along the way,

I got to know her a little more. I learned that her parents were farmers. My colleague referred to herself as a farm girl. She also mentioned some of her childhood friends who, like her, were also farm girls. She was raised, grew up on a dairy farm, and learned farming from her parents. Later, when she went to university, she took agriculture.

After her studies, she went back to the farm and worked for her parents. As her parents were aging, she got more and more control of the family business. Of course, later, her parents retired, and she got full control. At this point, she managed to grow the farm by buying more land.

Today she is a considerably wealthy woman. During and after this conversation, I could not help but realize how this woman built on something she already had at her disposal. It might have taken her more work to be as successful as she has been if she chose to follow a different career path, like, for example, politics.

RELATIONSHIP

*A*s adults, the two most important things that are a consistent part of our lives are our careers and our relationships. This is because they go hand in hand in shaping our lives and our future.

When we talk about relationships, we are talking about love and courtship in this context. As young and emerging adults, relationships are a constant in our lives. We are at the mark or point in our lives where we continuously crave attention and love, which leads us to always seeking to start a relationship with someone we think could make us happy.

There are simply two types of relationships people can end up with: **Positive** and **negative connections**.

Relationships are part of adulthood, and it is a criterion for developing and establishing social relationships, among others. It brings about a sense of identity that is important for adults, especially among emerging adulthood. Sometimes, these relationships can be long-lasting, and at other times, they end up sourly. Why, then, are relationships meaningful as part of maturity?

Tina Stone

> *I grew up in a loving home where I was the only child and had both parents' love and attention. For sixteen years of my life, I thought I had the ideal family till one afternoon, I got back from school and saw my mother crying. My parents were getting a divorce because they both were unhappy with each other.*
>
> *My whole world was shattered, and I felt betrayed for a long time because I felt I had been living a lie. That, in a way, changed how I viewed relationships, and for a long time, I did not see the need to get into one. Even while in college, I had flings, but I never wanted anything serious to do with anyone. I*

always thought of my parents, and the thought that usually came to my mind was, **why are relationships so important to people knowing that they would both end up hurting?**

Relationships are an essential aspect and part of growing up to be responsible adults and, in the long run, prepare us for marriage and parenthood. Relationships are critical for young adults because they significantly influence our self-esteem and bring about a sense of belonging.

Sadly, a lot of young people are satisfied with being in toxic relationships nowadays. They prefer the type of relationship that thrives on public attention, sex, and other unhealthy vices. Nobody wants to spend time having a quality type of relationship that is value-driven, and that is where the problem starts. We should all strive for a healthy relationship.

A healthy relationship can boost one's confidence and promote overall physical and mental health and improve social skills. In contrast, a problematic relationship can hurt a person's emotional, psychological, and even physical health, making one very unhappy.

A positive relationship builds everyone for the future by improving and encouraging each other to solidify and maintain long-lasting friendships with people outside the relationship.

A positive relationship has the following benefits to both partners, and they are:

- A positive relationship acts as a support mechanism for couples because they can seek support from their partners, especially during hard and challenging times.

I cannot help but feel comfortable whenever I speak to my friend about certain things, especially when it comes to emotional issues affecting me. She has a way of comforting me with her words. It is like she is a guardian angel of some sort. And to be honest, I do not know what I would do without her sometimes.

— OWEN

- A positive relationship also inspires one to seek personal growth. When you are honest and healthy, your partner usually encourages you to achieve your own goals and objectives. A good relationship seeks individuals to flourish and have their accomplishments.

I always knew I was a good writer, but I lacked the confidence to go ahead and own a blog, one of my life-long dreams. However, I had to tell my friend about it, and he encouraged me to start up a blog and even pursue a career as a professional writer. It was so beautiful how he believed in me and that alone made me want to do my best. Today, I own my blog, and I am a professional writer for others. I would never have been ever able to do all of this without the encouragement of my friend.

— LEANNA

- Another benefit of seeking a healthy and positive relationship is that it rubs off on others around and extends to your immediate circle. A positive relationship influences not just you but also your family and friends and how you relate with them.

My son used to be a very temperamental child while growing up. Billy could get angry over the littlest of things, and being with him was like walking on eggshells because you never knew when he could switch and become an angry 'beast.'

One summer vacation, he showed up at the family dinner with a pretty girl he introduced to us as his friend. It was intriguing because she looked so fragile that we did not think she would be able to stand any of Billy's tantrums.

However, we were shocked to see that Billy no longer reacted to things the way he used to because she had a way of calming him down in ways we never could. Suddenly, being with him was not such a scary thing as we now rest assured that we could crack a joke around him without unleashing a whirlwind of angry emotions.

— BETTY

- A positive relationship offers both partners an opportunity to do all that they want to do, therefore adding meaning and purpose to the lives of both parties involved. It brings about a stronger sense of identity and gives every action you take an extra meaning.

I have had the most fantastic experience with my friend. Every day we learn new things about each other. Everything is so beautiful and effortless with her. I could say that I am blown away by someone who once did not believe in me, and the help I get when I am with her is something I will always cherish.

— CLINTON

- A positive relationship enables you to be more accountable to your partners. In turn, it allows you to build and showcase a level of responsibility and accountability to others around you, especially family members.

Being with my friend of five years, it already feels like I am a married man. I know that sounds hilarious, but that is how I think. It is like I am now programmed towards being responsible and accountable to her and my family.

Every decision I take is something I do while bearing her emotions and contribution in mind. She has shaped me to be a more responsible young man, and I must acknowledge that she is incredible. Do not be put off by what people say. There is still something nice about being in a relationship.

— BARRY

Relationships among adults can be exciting as well as challenging too. Some issues may sometimes arise in these relationships, and most of them are bordered on sex, one-sided relationships, cheating, and other insecurities that may play out among partners.

However, we should understand that these issues can be avoided, but finding different ways to sort these issues out if they do happen is essential. One of the best ways to go about this is through **effective communication.** Learn to talk things out with your partner and trash whatever issues you have. Always learn to talk things out. It brings about a level of understanding and tolerance among both partners.

Another way is by developing **mutual respect**. When in a relationship, one must respect their partner's ideas and input in whatever they discuss or embark on. Consideration is one of the essential attributes of a positive relationship, and both individuals need to realize and value this factor.

A healthy and positive relationship cannot stand without trust. **Trust** is the most significant deciding factor in any relationship, and individuals need to develop confidence in their relationship with each other. Everyone who has been in a long-lasting relationship can attest that trust is the most incredible foundation of any relationship.

Recently, this trend among young people feeling the need to show off their social media relationship. They want people to tag them as the 'picture perfect' couple. While this is not such a terrible idea, a relationship that thrives on social media has a very high probability of breaking than one that is out of the public's eyes. You must understand that once you start to view and listen to people's opinions on how your relationship should be, unknowingly, you begin to streamline whatever actions you take in your relationship, according to these public opinions.

You do not have to be swayed by what people put up before you. No relationship is ideal or perfect, and there is no relationship without issues. Quarrels are bound to occur, but it is essential to **be mindful** of the things we say to each other.

Contrary to popular belief, words do have a massive influence on how the relationship plays out. Words can make or break a relationship, so it is necessary for friends always to mind the words they utter to themselves, especially in a heated argument, because these words have a way of sticking and setting the victim off.

Relationships will always be a part of growing up. These will shape us and supply us with the experiences we need to know, primarily as they concern our emotional maturity. Therefore, young adults need to understand how these relationships work and how they will benefit them before venturing into one.

These emotional experiences we get from relationships are usually geared towards preparing us for marital life and coping with the challenges to come. Relationships can be a horrifying experience for everyone, especially when you get into a toxic and negative one. It can scar you, but it is geared towards teaching lessons, and we all must aspire to make all our relationships positive relationships. And this shouldn't just be with friends, but in the work/social relationships we have with other people.

We cannot talk about young adulthood without talking about relationships, managing their emotions, and even treating their relationships. Some individuals have been so affected by their previous relationships that they unconsciously offload these negative emotions on their new relationship. It is not supposed to be that way.

For a long time, I was an extremely wary fiancée *who never trusted her* fiancé *because I thought he would cheat one day. My previous relationships always had, for some weird reason ended with the guy cheating on me.*

When I got into this new relationship, I was very skeptical about his activities and was always alert whenever I saw his phone ring or when he told me he was going out with friends. Of course, I have never openly confronted him about it, but I fed off on my paranoia, and it started to affect our relationship. It was only when he threatened to break up with me that I realized that I needed to work on myself. Together we have both been to a counselor, and I do not always feel that way anymore. And with each day, I am learning to let go of past experiences and spare my partner the trouble.

— CATHERINE

The relationship is not about sex or what you define as love. Relationships are the stepping ground in which you can become a better person and, most importantly, a better husband or wife.

Therefore, young people need to model other positive relationships around them, especially close family members.

BALANCING CAREER AND
RELATIONSHIP

---

*T*ime. There never seems to be enough.

There are relationships, career, personal interest, family, and social demands, all screaming for attention in our life. All of us have the same amount of time available to us as we begin a new day. Twenty-four hours to use or abuse as we see fit.

This is not a book about time management. Time management is a misnomer. You cannot manage time. Time passes, oblivious to your needs, desires, problems, goals, expectations, and dreams. You can only manage a variety of activities and attitudes within a framework of passing the time. Well, if we cannot manage time, what can we handle? We can control our resources, decisions, thoughts, expectations, challenges, people, failures, activities, successes, risks, feelings, goals, money, emotions, and a whole host of attitudes.

Let us get to the heart of the issue. Many people live with daily frustration, unable to effectively manage some or all the items on the previous list. They are anxious, troubled, and often angry at the relentless passage of time-insensitive to their wishes, demands, frustrations, and goals.

Many of these people feel stuck, have given up, or have settled, thinking, this is just the way it is and must be. They see themselves as a pawn to the demands and expectations of one or more areas of their life, therefore, robbing themselves of the pleasure and happiness available to everyone who has learned to live with balance.

These people are out of balance, and they know it. They feel like their life is out of control. They feel stuck. They see themselves with very few options. They do not realize that the choices that they have made in the past determine their next opportunities. Because of poor decisions in the present, there will also be equally limited options for a better future. Yes, we all always have choices, but if these choices are made with a narrow vision of what can be, an unclear picture of reality, or clouded perceptions and interpretations of people and circumstances, they will always be made with limited resources and under-standing.

These people remain stuck. Some have moved on in some areas of their life, but they still feel unable to shed the feelings of anxiety that there is more to do, more to become, more to have, and more to learn, and not enough time to do it.

Several significant areas in a person's life demand a portion of their available time. They are family, career or business, social, personal development, spiritual development, physical development, personal inter-ests or hobbies, friends, misc. Social activities, and let us not forget time to sleep and eat.

Is it possible to live a balanced life? Is it possible to satisfy the expectations of how we should be using our time? Is it possible to have it all? Become it all? Do it all? See it all? Learn it all? Read it all? No, it is not that kind of world.

So, we are back to a choice. How each of us decides to use or spend our time is an individual matter? Juggling the expectations of a boss, customers, spouse, children, parents, friends, siblings, and the world, in general, is a challenging and delicate task at best. No one has all the answers or easy formulas to this complicated life issue, but as the bible has it all, we only need to use it as our life manual and apply the instructions we get as we daily discover the right path. You will not find all answers in this book. What I hope you will find, however, is some insight or discovery as to why you feel as you are—the courage to modify any behavior or attitudes that are sabotaging one or several areas of your life.

You may have noticed that when one area of your life is out of harmony or balance that it impacts every other place as well. When you are devoting too much time (and only you know what is too much) to your career, every other aspect of your life is impacted. Every part of your life is intricately entwined with every other area. If you choose to devote no time to your personal growth, you will lack the skill, understanding, or wisdom to contribute positively to some other aspect of your life. By the same token, if you spend time regularly relaxing or meditating, it will help you find the patience or calmness that you will bring to your career or family issues.

Why do people get out of balance?

Several causes include but are not limited to:

unrealistic goals or a lack of goals, lack of planning, a need for approval and acceptance, inadequate personal growth, overestimation of abilities or skills, the inability to say no, the desire to please, lack of discipline, arrogance, greed, insensitivity, lack of spiritual development, un-managed ambition, the need for power, unchecked egos, lack of commitment and a lack of unity or integrity. Hefty list. I would guess that everyone who is out of balance in their lives is guilty of several of them. Being out of balance in life does not feel right.

Life is lived in the present, one moment at a time. It is not lived yesterday or tomorrow, but now. Every time you decide to spend time in a certain way, like spending time reading this book, you have eliminated all other choices of time used now. Once you choose to go to a movie, you have eliminated the options of dinner, dancing, golf, and so on. Once you decide to work late, you have chosen to sacrifice something else. I do not mean to be hilarious, but you cannot be in two places at once. You cannot be on vacation and at work too, although many people try. Once you choose one restaurant for dinner, you have eliminated all others for that meal.

People need to understand that they have choices and that their choices and consequences are a part of the bargain. Frustration sometimes sneaks into people's lives when they believe it is possible to break the rules, have it all, do it all, or become it.

You chose your career and life path. You chose your current relationship. You chose your current circumstances by the previous choices you have made. You made them for yourself. Even if you are in a career that was chosen for you by your parents (and that happens less and less today than years ago), you have chosen to stay in it even if you are unhappy. You have given the power in your life over to someone else.

If you rationalize that you must work eighty hours a week and weekends because your boss or organization expects it, you have given up your power to someone else. Then you might say, but I need this job or career. I need the money. No, you have chosen to need it. You could have chosen a different, more modest lifestyle that would have required less income. Like it or not, you are where you are because of your choices in every situation in life. Do you want a better life? Then you must make different choices.

I would like to share fifteen ideas with you that may help you put balance back into your life to find time for the people and goals in your life that are possibly being shortchanged, including yourself.

1. Spend some quiet time reflecting on the quality of your life in general. Not just a single area, but consider every aspect and the relationship of each to your overall life.

2. Make a list of all the areas or people in your life coming up short and why.

3. Determine which area of your life is getting most of your time and energy and which is getting the least. Ask yourself why. Is the gain in one place worth paying the price of a loss in another area? Only you can answer that question, and only you will pay the price or enjoy the rewards.

4. Write a letter to yourself about how you would like your life to look six months from now. Describe how you spend your time and what proportions of time are dedicated to your life's various activities and people.

5. Give yourself at least thirty minutes a day for thirty days to reflect on your overall life goals and your progress toward them.

6. Write a personal mission statement. Include your life values, guiding principles, desired outcomes, and the overall direction you want your life to take.

7. Move ahead mentally to age 70. What have you accomplished, what do your relationships look like, who have you become, and what is important to you? Now work backward. What do you need to change to get to where you would want to be? Remember, you have to change the quality of your future in the present.

8. Ask several people who know you well and be honest and nonjudgmental to offer feedback on your life and its direction. Listen and learn with an open and receptive attitude. You may not change because of the feedback they give you, but the insight you gain can give you some ideas that could be life-changing.

9. Take a few days off from your job, career, and current relationships. Spend time in a place that you are at peace and alone. It

could be the beach, the mountains, or anywhere where you can spend quality time with yourself evaluating your life without the distractions and expectations of others. Go with no agenda other than a discovery.

10. If you do not keep a journal of your thoughts, lessons learned, life progress, feelings, interests, or observations, start one today. Take a few minutes at the end of each day recording whatever you feel in some way contributed to who you are, how you think, and whom you are becoming in character.

11. Develop an action plan to re-allocate your time and energy to those people or activities important to you.

12. It is unnecessary to sell your business and quit your job to find a better balance in your life. It requires a conscious awareness of what your life is really like, a desire to modify it somehow, the courage to change, the necessary skills, and the commitment to stick with it.

13. Learn to detach from other people's emotional and or physical hold over you. It will not be easy. There will be people who use blame, guilt, manipulation, or any

number of emotional or biological techniques to keep you stuck in past behavior or thought patterns. They will know how to push your buttons, hoping to control you in some way. When you permit others to manipulate you in any way, you give them power over your life. Detachment means letting go of the hold other people have over you. You can still love them and want to be with them, but you no longer must be a slave to their "stuff."

14. Don't try and change everything over-night. It takes time to change attitudes and behavior that have developed over the years. One thing that changed the earth initially was when God spoke to it, and it is still the same way our lives can be turned around when God's word says to our lives. Be patient and loving with yourself. But you must also hold yourself accountable. Letting yourself off the hook or making excuses will not put you on the road back to a balanced life.

15. Reward your effort. Treat yourself when you achieve a "worked for" result. Make it something symbolic or significant, but whatever it is, make sure you take time to bask in the sunshine of success. Then begin

again. Do not spend too much time basking, or you may fall back into your old habits. Change, permanent change requires vigilance and persistence. You cannot let up until you have achieved total and permanent success. It will always be possible to fall back, so even though you have reached your goal, do not become too casual or relaxed. There will be new people and circumstances lurking in the shadows for a vulnerable moment. Be watchful.

None of these steps may be easy. Only you can decide if the potential outcome of more balance and inner peace is worth the price that must be paid. Do not change because of guilt, other people's expectations, or some casual or superficial whim. If you like working twenty hours a week and seeing your kids every day for a few hours. Fine. If you want to change, that is fine too. But do it for healthy convictions, emotional or physical reasons, not ego-driven motives.

FALLING IN LOVE WITH A CAREER YOU DO NOT HAVE

It is not just relationships that are unrequited. Some are spiritual and purely based on ambition and passion. A perfect example is falling in love with a career that you do not have.

Busy people spend at least eight hours per day all over the whole week. Perhaps you might be going to school for the same duration. Employed individuals and students who are always busy with activities that they need to do. Because of this, you might think of a job that you have wanted to achieve for so many years now. This excessive infatuation level might not even help you reach that dream job, but instead, it distracts you from success.

The question is, how can you address this potentially-breaking situation? Here are a few precise actions you can do if you are in love with a job you do not have.

Recognize what makes you demotivated.

If you have enjoyed your work or school time before, but now you wake up in terror of walking out of the house, consider the possible reasons you feel demotivated. Maybe you have had something going on with your life in your household, and it is going to make your job difficult. You might be working so hard. Still, it sounds like it is getting overlooked.

If you felt obsessed with a job that you have always wanted, ask yourself. You might think it is challenging to make every morning and know if you will be searching for a brand-new career tonight. However, before you offer your notice, try to explain what makes you mad – are you getting bored, demotivated, or feeling something even more profound?

Create a list of drawbacks

Consider what you should do with them to change the condition or fix the dilemma. Create another set of new projects to get them to partner with you. Hold them as a list of the little improvements you would like to see, and then start going on them or speak to somebody who might be willing to listen and assist you.

Actively alter what worries you

When you understand what makes you sad, you will pinpoint the core of the problem. Over the summer months, we all slip into unproductivity. For example, while other colleagues are on break, looking out at the bright outdoors, pinching an ice-cold pint in the garden. No one wants to go to work at this period. Yet we must pay the bills, and we need to show up. So, if you are upset at your workplace, you should be looking out for how you can make a difference.

Take a well-deserved rest

Give yourself a break. Take a well-deserved rest after a stressful week. Book a vacation, take a few days to hang out, or go for a short staycation, and make sure to reflect on you from your maker's perspective. Feel free to turn off your email alerts, and set aside all your work-related feelings for a while. Enjoy your day-off, and that will likely make you feel refreshed.

The outcome of getting obsessed with a job that you do not have is inconsistency. So, as a career aspirant, consider the recommendations mentioned above to avoid rushing things. Planning before taking any action always pays off.

HOW TO DEAL WITH CHANGES
IN LIFE

———————— ❦ ————————

*T*he one constant thing in life is change. That does not mean we get used to it or fully embrace it, though. Several adults have grown to become unchanging, considering their mindsets. Many graduates would have conditioned their perspectives on what they should expect from society-job, housing, car, etc. immediately after they graduate. But when such did not come as expected, they end up committing suicide or losing their lives to depression and worries, culminating in them becoming mentally unstable.

After Stan graduated from university, he anticipated that he should get called up for an interview. A few months before his graduation, he had had his resume submitted in various establishments. Weeks strolled by, and nothing came forth from those establishments. He felt they might have forgotten though he was told, then they would get back to him.

His endless wait amounted to nothing. Weeks became months and months gradually became years. As all these continued, a pile of pressure gathered on him, and all he could think of was **SUICIDE**.

What do you think was responsible for Stan's death? Do you think it was the job that was not forthcoming? No! He was the architect of his predicament, and he knew he failed in that regard. What was that supposed to mean? He was not evolving with society. He believed the community was a ready-made environment that will hand over to him whatever his desires were. He underestimated the power of his ability to think and create something out of nothing.

When life does not give you what you demand, that is a change. Thus, you need to understand that life itself wants you, at that very moment, to change the situation around. Remember, opportunity does not come to you by chance or luck. You create an opportunity for yourself.

Had Mark Zuckerberg dropped out of Harvard only

to fall prey to the hands of depression, he would not have stunned the world today as the youngest billionaire from his creation of Facebook. Another person would have achieved that feat, and that would have amounted to loss on his part. Think outside of the box and grant or allow yourself to revolve around life.

Some people believe that the kind of life they live is due to the career they have chosen. While this can be true to them, those of a different view regarding this see life differently from a job.

What is there in life after a career? To be honest, True life is not a career but the example of life that Jesus came to live and show us as humans to follow, and as we live that life, we come into real life.

Knowledge of God, which we get when we read his word, plus obedience to what has been read and heard, equals a life that practically releases inner life to us as humans.

One of the major issues that teachers and other educational professionals are facing today is this. Let us face it. Anybody who has been in an education career ten years or more especially will tell you, almost consistently, that their view of practice and their role in it has changed dramatically over what it once was even a few short years ago.

Of course, some of this is just a shift in different attitudes as we age, but in my opinion, some of this also is deeply rooted in the number of challenges that we are faced with, with ever-increasing frequency. The more challenges you face determines how far you would go in life, so enjoy it. When circumstances change, you also change to cope with them.

Well, I hope you see where I am going here. Are you going through the "changes"? Somehow, years have passed since graduation, and life is not quite what you had imagined.

One of the significant consequences of this that I see every day in counseling is people in their early 30s to mid-50s who have a challenging time producing the fun and fulfillment in their work that not too long ago seemed natural and comfortable.

With all this said, I have some practical suggestions.

Evaluate Your Level of Control

Sometimes it is all too effortless to become fixated on events over which we have no power, capacity, or people who might never change their actions or attitude. But rather than focus on attributing blames to others or moving, the unmovable, resilient individuals set their sights on what they can control. To assess and evaluate your level of control over a situation, you can ask or challenge yourself, "What can I take responsibility for in this situation?" When you notice or look for opportunities to empower yourself and work towards a possible change, you are less likely to sense or feel stuck in difficult and challenging positions.

Practice Self-Care After a Loss

Often, life's transitions involve losses, such as a death, a big move, the loss of a job, or a relationship ending. Even positive shifts, like a convocation or a job change, can make you feel heartbroken. During these times of transition, do not push away any agony you might feel. Acknowledge the loss or disaster, and pay attention to what you have learned and gained from experience.

Seek support and camaraderie among colleagues, friends, and family, and consider speaking with a counselor or other mental health professional if you feel you need extra help during the transition.

Check Your Thought Patterns

In times of change, it is easy for your mind to cut corners. You might see everything in black and white, or you presume the worst will occur. But if you take the time to ponder and examine your thought patterns and assess how rational they are, you might find some space to nudge your thinking towards resilience. If you are not sure how to slow down your mind, practicing relaxation techniques, such as mindfulness or deep breathing, can help you feel more in control of your brain and how you evaluate a significant change transition.

You can also generate more conclusive positive reflective thoughts if you take the time to remember and remind yourself about the transitions and challenges you successfully navigated in the past. Make a list of ways you have been resilient in your life, and consider what peculiarity, traits, and actions might be able to see you through the current test or challenge. Focusing on your energy and strengths instead of your weaknesses will make you feel more empowered to meet what lies ahead.

Be in the Present

While it is essential to look to the past to find your

vigor, strengths, sometimes you can feel too pulled into the future in times of change. When you are apprehensive or worry about what the future will bring or what mistakes you might make, you forget to be present and observe what is happening around you. To bring yourself back to the now, get in tune with your body. Pay consideration to how it responds to stress, and set aside time every day to relax, take some deep breaths, and bring your focus back to the present.

Find Your Priorities

The most resilient individuals see change as an opportunity rather than a beast or monster to fear. Transitions in life avow you to consider where your priorities lie. How do you want to use your time on earth? What is essential to you? Where do you see yourself dissipating your time and energy? With a clear crystal sense of your goals and values, you will find your mind and body more resilient when changing stressors.

Above all, you prioritize your health in life's transitions meaning not being afraid to ask for help when you need it. Human beings are social creatures by essence and nature, so you were not built to withstand every sudden event in life without others' support. Talk to friends and families experiencing similar changes, or consider finding a support group in your community. Ask your doctor about prioritizing your health during the transition and not being afraid to talk to a counselor or other health professional about building resilience. You cannot avoid change, but you can live a life of stability. You can embrace transition and see tests or challenges as opportunities to thrive.

TIPS ON HOW TO CONQUER AND SUBDUE THE FEAR OF A NEW LIFE

The idea of starting over is both exciting and fearful. Exciting because you get to begin again, but with the knowledge and skills you already have in your arsenal. On the other hand, the fear part is usually because starting over is still full of uncertainties. If you are the anxious kind, then you probably feel the latter more.

Fear of the unknown is a natural body response when faced with something that feels uncertain, and it is entirely normal. However, succumbing to the fear of starting a new life can also result in you not living your best life. You absolutely would not want to miss those opportunities, and we are here to encourage you to take a leap of faith.

Here are tips on how to overcome the fear of starting a new life:

- **Look back at your motivation**. Each person has their respective reasons for why they want to begin a new life. Whether it is a job opportunity outside the country or something else, knowing the root of your new-life decision will determine what changes or improvements you want to see. Similarly, those experiences you want to change in your life will give you courage and push you to start over.

- **Envision the future you want**. The underlying motivation to your decision to start fresh should not only exist to jumpstart your decision. Instead, you should always have the outcome you want in your head. It will be easy to distract someone not working in the service of a dream. Set your achievable and time-bound goals in building that future you want, then always envision these results. Knowing the path to take is but a single step, but knowing where to go will make your walk into the new life clearer. That is less of the fears now.

- **Accept the fact that failures happen**. There is no point in lying to yourself and denying it anyway. Nor will we advise that "you will not fail" but "fear not because failures are not painful." They will happen, and they do hurt. But accepting that they exist and preparing yourself for the worst possible case scenario lessens the fears of starting over. Aside from this, you can devise ways to prevent it from happening.

- **There is no growth in comfort zones**. Creating a new life is not only exciting but even more challenging. It is like entering a decision-making game, but you are the main protagonist. This is what makes life exciting - the challenge of living. When you get comfortable, you become stagnant. You become used to your complacent and sedentary lifestyle. Life is thrilling when there are challenges. You get to know more of yourself when you are exposed outside your box.

Yes, it is a scary and uncertain decision. But taking it may be life-changing if you learn to calculate and assess the pros and cons of every scenario. Do not be afraid of starting new. You will do great, and we believe in you!

HOW TO PULL YOURSELF TOGETHER AFTER FAILING

Failure is painful and inevitable. Sooner or later, you will come to realize that you are not the best, even in your field of expertise. But will this reality get in the way of your path to success? If there is one truth, you must realize that the road to success is anything but smooth. There will always be bumps. There will always be slumps. It will hurt your ego, but then again, will a hurt ego stop you?

Take it from Oprah Winfrey. She said, "failure is another stepping stone to greatness." And she is entirely accurate. Failure is the best teacher, after all. Remember that being defeated or failing is not the end of your journey. It merely means you did not get it right the first time.

Getting back on track depends heavily on how you handle the failure. You can simply sit back, cry, and let it paralyze your being, or you can stand up and continue fighting. Everything is in your hands. But we are glad to give you a helping hand in your time of defeat. With that in mind, here are a few tips on how to pull yourself after failing:

- **Accept the truth.** There is no point in denying that you lost the battle. Accept the truth. It begins there. You failed now, but it is not the end of the world. Failing is okay, and failing today is not definitive of what will happen tomorrow. If so, then we would not have met Steve Jobs, Bill Gates, JK Rowling, Jack Ma, and a long list of failures turned into the world's most successful people.

- **Do not pin the blame on anyone.** The most common defense mechanism people do to cope with loss is looking for other people to blame. The truth of the matter is, the only one to blame is yourself. Take full responsibility for the failure. If you keep blaming others, then it is like having your success depends on them. Success and failure are in your hands.

- **Identify where you went wrong.** Whatever materialized in the past can no longer be redone and reversed. But we can always learn from the past. Get as much information from your failure. What were your weaknesses, and what were your strengths? List them down and hone the areas where you think you lacked effort. Remember that it is "pulling yourself" from failure, which means that it is an active process. You do not remain in your broken state, but you press on toward the goal despite the brokenness. You do things that will improve yourself.

- **Toughen yourself from the setbacks.** As Rudy Francisco puts it, "muscle is created by repeatedly lifting things that have been designed to weigh us down." Every time you get back up from failing, remember that you become more challenging, healthier, and better. Soon enough, you will shrug off every failure you get and come backpacking a more potent punch.

Failure is a part of life. It adds to the thrill of living, and if we do not learn to step out of our comfort zones, then it is like we are not even living at all. Triumph at every success and learn from every failure, but do not ever stay where you are as of now. Always push to be at the top.

s an adult, you are definitely in search of progress, right? So why not make it as simple as possible? Use these eight straightforward steps right now to put yourself on the path to achieving what you want in a short amount of time.

There are many frameworks for progress out there, but what works for you is not always what works for everyone else. Here is how you can apply the categories of passion, work, focus, push, ideas, improve, serve, persist, and balance as adults.

Passion

This area rarely seems to be a problem for adults. They have more trouble trying to limit or narrow down their passions than they do try to find one in the first place.

So as far as passion goes, select the one that stands out the most for you right now and thinks about what you could do to make it neat, impactful, and bump on the world.

This zeal will be one foundational piece of your fun dental mission - the path that will give you the ultimate excitement, pleasure, and satisfaction in life. You will possibly find that many of your great and impactful passions will fit together to formulate your essential mission entirely over time. And when that happens, you will be in an incredible place!

Work

However, you would like to consider it. It will take a lot of work to get to the climax of your life experience and involvement. Time, sweat, effort, money, and tears are all involved here.

The essential thing to remember as you are putting in vast amounts of effort, and being gifted, are likely on an emotional roller coaster for a good part of the time, is that every step of the way is getting you closer to where you want to be. Even if it does not look related to it, or if everyone around you is telling you that you are wasting your time, know that every learning experience makes you a more knowledgeable and more robust person who can handle the progress that comes at the top.

Focus

The things that you yen for in life will not necessarily drop into your lap - you will have to work for them - but you'll find that they will all come together much more quickly when you've determined your focus or focal point. You know for sure, or at minimum, mostly for sure, what you are aspiring for. (Not having a fixate focus is kind of like deciding to go on holiday but not knowing where. When you choose your destination, it makes getting there a whole lot easier.)

For adults, finding focus means doing one thing very well and figuring out how to use the many things you do well to make a difference in the lives of yourself and others. It is not about narrowing your focus down to such a point that it includes only one thing. It is about combining your many compass issues to create something new, exciting, and unexplored.

Push

This is one of the utmost trying parts of the process for gifted adults. Usually, the aims they have in life are not the traditional ones that most individuals shoot for. The things that bring them the most peace of mind are what may not be understood by many of the individuals closest to them. So, what do they do? This is where making connections with other skilled and gifted grownups are mandatory.

It is tough enough to progress at doing ordinary things, so you must set up your support systems in a big way when you are ready to move at an ultimate unconventional level. When you begin to feel down and out, when the work is becoming overwhelming, or when you feel like you are not even sure you are on the right track, getting in touch with your gifted friends can offer you the push you so definitely need that moment in time.

Ideas

Generating objectives and ideas is also something that usually comes relatively easy for gifted grownups. The challenge or test for them is to figure out which ones to use right now and which ones to place on the back burner for a while.

Keeping a journal or note is very helpful for this, as it will be having some tremendous let's-bang-around-some-great-ideas discussions with gifted friends. You can use or adapt some local or reachable experts in the fields you are working with, which will refine your reflections and insights. And suppose independent, do-it-now kind of idea creation is what you prefer. In that case, you can try setting up a filing cabinet with folders or compartments for each of your magnificent ideas, along with the supplies they need to put them into action.

Improve

This one more given for many gifted grownups. You can say it or have it built-in directly somehow. For them, the desire to reform and revamp is less like a potential option and more like a life-giving necessity.

Sometimes, for adults, the desire to improve is so strong that what to do or how to go about it in the best way becomes more of a challenge. Using the connections you have made with positive and uplifting people will help you figure out where the most important places are for you to progress from the position you are standing in right now. And recall, with the high learning curve that giftedness brings, your area of improvement might be different tomorrow, and next week, and next month. Just know that it is OK.

Serve

This is one extra area that's nearly part of adults' genetic makeup - the need to give something besides themselves. The undisclosed for them is to put their unique sets of passions together to create something that maximally serves others.

You can do amazing things; you have got bucket loads of ideas and passions; you are not afraid to keep on trying, and you want to help individuals with what you do. So now scrutinize what you would love to do, be and have if you had all the space, money, and resources you needed at your fingertips, and then take the first traces toward making that real. Putting the pieces together to adjust the world, not just in any way, but most beneficially and positively, is the goal now.

Persist

Isn't it surprising that one of the critical traits of gift-edness is also one of the eight keys to success?

The biggest challenge for adults here is not that they are not persistent - they so often are to an incredible degree - but that they keep moving forward when they are feeling down and out when the world goes against them and when their unconventional concept is just beginning to emerge into the conceptualizations of the rest of the planet. -- So perhaps the ultimate success question for gifted adults is this: If 6-7 of these secrets to success are built into them, why are they not all incredibly successful?

The most significant answer lies in Progress Point 4 - Push. At only 3-5% of the general population, grown-ups are so physically scattered in their cities, communities, and countries that they have trouble finding one another. And without other people who under-stand their intensities and what some may call insani-ties, it is hard to keep moving forward.

If you are a grown-up, be on the lookout for others like you anywhere and everywhere you go. And when you find them, hang onto them, especially the positive, motivating ones, because their presence around you may just be the final piece you need to complete the puzzle of your essential life mission and find ultimate progress.

Balance

Sometimes, you get caught up in chasing your dreams and passion, and it is not wrong. However, challenges arise when you fail to look over your personal life because you are too preoccupied with being the best in your field.

Too much work, no matter how noble the principle behind it, has negative repercussions. That is why a maintained life and work balance is essential. There must be time for work, but they're also must be allotted time for personal matters. Here are tips you can use to maintain your balance:

- **Assess your productivity schedule.** The first step starts from within. Know who you are. Are you a late-night owl or an early bird? By understanding the most productive period, you can assign the problematic tasks on that time frame and leave the relatively easy ones on the less productive hours. This way, your workload may be distributed according to your strengths and weaknesses.

- **Set a work period and strictly follow it**. It would be counter-intuitive to work office duties at night, so you are left with no other choice but to work during the day. By setting your mind to work on your 9-5 shift, you will be able to condition your body to be productive when your productivity needs it! This means more work was done during the day, with no overtime, and you can spend time with your family at home.

- **Learn to unplug when needed.** Work can be very stressful. Taking a breather is never wrong. If your work becomes too toxic and stressful, then take a step back and relax for a while. Grinding your head too much at work will diminish your enthusiasm and energy to continue. Unplugging from it for a while will not only be good for your mental and physical health, even more so, it will give you the positive vibe you need to get back to work after.

- **Be sure your health is at its best.** One common thing that lets you go off when one is swamped with work is exercising. Yes, your dues and deadlines are essential, but so is your health. When you postpone your evening jogs or weekend gyms, you only make room for stress to build in without releasing the tension. This will affect your life-work balance because there is no longer "life" flowing inside you. Take care of your health.

- **Make time for what matters most.** This tip goes both ways. Too much personal time leaves no room for work. On the other hand, too much work will burn you out. The information is about making time, not finding the time. Try to assess yourself. When you see an imbalance in your life schedule, make time for what matters most. Be it family, yourself, your friends, or even work if needed.

I remember an inspirational story that goes with our work-life balance topic.

The father was swamped with work and always went home late. He no longer had attention from his family. He then noticed his son continually asking for money from him. This system went on for some time. When the son collected enough, he gave it all back to his father and said: "Dad, this is equal to your salary. Can mom and I have your time for a month?" This broke him into tears and made him change his ways.

Work-life balance is essential. Check yourself. Maybe you are leaving something important behind.

PLEASE LEAVE A 1-CLICK REVIEW!

I hope you enjoyed reading this book!

If you haven't done so yet, I would be incredibly thankful if you could take 60 seconds to write a brief review on the platform of purchase, even if it's just a few sentences!

Your feedback will be a huge help in helping other readers benefit from the information in the book.

You can also contact us by sending an email to tcecpublishing@outlook.com

Like us on https://www.facebook.com/tcecpublishing/

Join our Facebook page : https://www.facebook.com/groups/800312427190446 to stay updated on our next releases!

See you there!

Your free gift!

Voucher ID: NGH0001

Download your free copy here

https://tcecpublishing.com/tcsf-free-ebook

CONCLUSION

Summing up, these are some of the ways you could take more responsibility in life. Taking all these steps mentioned in this book means that you are a mature adult. You do not let life go astray but stay healthy through the hard times without getting devastated and ruining yourself. Look out for the silver lining behind every cloud and be joyfully happy.

OTHER BOOKS YOU'LL LOVE!

REFERENCES

[1] https://www.selfgrowth.com/articles/Are_We_Adults.html

[2] https://www.dailyschoolnews.com.ng/score-high-in-post-utme/

[3] https://www.philosophytalk.org/shows/what-adult

[4] https://www.philosophytalk.org/blog/what-adult

[5] https://storybuilder.jumpstart.ge/en/sweet-voiced-cocodrile

[6] https://www.officialcharts.com/chart-news/looking-back-at-amy-winehouses-back-to-black-ten-10-years-on__15545/

[7]   https://www.forbes.com/sites/marcusnoel/2018/06/25/magnate-ceo-rustin-keller-is-transporting-human-wellness-values-to-gen-z/

[8]   https://fashionista.com/2019/04/natural-beauty-myths-claims-facts-debunked

[9]   https://teacher-blogdeaula.blogspot.com/2011_04_27_archive.html

[10] https://www.gilmorecommunication.com/results-level-2-combinations/

[11]   https://esmemes.com/i/jaxkie-ajaxkkkie-as-you-get-older-you-start-to-see-bf65d72b99054d9b97acad9c2e1fa530

[12]   https://www.webmd.com/mental-health/depersonalization-disorder-mental-health

[13]   https://www.mentalhelp.net/blogs/self-responsibility-self-accountability-qualifies-you-as-an-adult/

[14]   https://www.newportfire.net/2020/06/16/four-things-that-can-help-you-advance-in-your-career/

[15]   https://laborworks.com/tips-to-prepare-for-a-new-job-or-career/

[16]   https://www.forbes.com/sites/francesbridges/ 2019/03/29/5-ways-to-be-a-more-positive-person/

[17]   https://www.geico.com/information/life-stages/ on-your-own/financial-responsibility-tips/

[18]   https://www.stevepavlina.com/blog/2005/01/ what-is-your-career/

[19]   https://www.dubaicareerguide.com/uae-career-tips/what-exactly-is-your-career.htm

[20] https://crazzyjob.blogspot.com/

[21]   https://campbell-north.com/blog/05-june-2018/ graduate-advice-%E2%80%93-how-get-job-you-actually-want

[22]   https://www.youtern.com/thesavvyintern/index. php/2013/09/15/in-3-steps-make-your-career-ah-ha-moment-happen/

[23]   https://govalor.com/story/leading-well-in-tough-times/

[24]   https://www.pickthebrain.com/11-important-things-know/

[25]   https://perfectpracticeweb.com/going-through-the-changes/

[26] https://31baa9204011a4b7373d-4b45c627b478904b4d98bc32b4be9291.ssl.cf2.rackcdn.com/uploaded/c/0e10020884_1585084882_counseling-corner-psychology-of-copng-with-change-3-20.pdf

[27] https://www.erikamohssen-beyk.com/better-mind/6-effective-ways-to-cope-with-big-changes/

[28] https://kuulpeeps.com/2019/05/24/uew-here-are-tips-on-how-to-overcome-the-exam-fear/kuulife

[29] https://www.happierhuman.com/use-affirmations/

[30] https://medium.com/synapse/the-first-five-years-lessons-learned-from-five-years-of-teaching-cad6401ea7d7

[31] https://www.marcandangel.com/2014/02/16/15-things-you-must-give-up-to-be-happy-again/

[32] https://blogs.findlaw.com/in_house/2018/11/businesswomen-who-failed-then-won.html

[33] http://blog.learnleo.com/passing-the-bar/

[34] https://personalitybuzz.com/are-you-an-early-bird-or-a-night-owl/

[35] https://www.dumblittleman.com/how-to-overcome-failure/

[36] https://businessbrokendown.com/2016/01/18/how-to-motivate-yourself-in-times-of-failure/

[37] https://www.success.com/13-inspiring-quotes-about-failure/

[38] https://build.wanderingaimfully.com/blog/fear-of-starting-something-new

[39] https://www.powerofpositivity.com/therapists-explain-6-ways-to-overcome-the-fear-of-starting-again/

[40] https://curlsandcocoa.com/how-to-start-a-new-life/

[41] https://www.lifecoach-directory.org.uk/blog/2017/08/07/5-things-when-out-of-love-with-job

[42] https://projecteve.com/12-signs-that-youve-fallen-out-of-love-with-career/

[43] https://www.businessnewsdaily.com/5244-improve-work-life-balance-today.html

[44] https://www.roche.com/careers/our-locations/asia/india/service/folder/20_tips_for_maintain.htm

[45]   https://www.forbes.com/sites/deborahlee/2014/10/20/6-tips-for-better-work-life-balance/#3e762f0229ff

[46]   https://www.skillsyouneed.com/ps/work-life-balance.html